The Ha

This Armada book belongs to:

Other Linda Craig® Mysteries in Armada

1 The Palomino Mystery
2 The Clue on the Desert Trail
3 The Secret of Rancho del Sol
4 The Mystery of Horseshoe Canyon
5 The Mystery in Mexico
6 The Ghost Town Treasure
8 The Secret of the Old Sleigh

LINDA CRAIG®

The Haunted Valley

ANN SHELDON

Illustrated by St Ward

Armada

First published in the U.S.A. in 1982
by Wanderer Books,
A Simon & Schuster Division of Gulf & Western Corporation.
First published in the U.K. in Armada in 1983 by
Fontana Paperbacks, 8 Grafton Street, London W1X 3LA

Printed in Great Britain by
William Collins Sons & Co. Ltd, Glasgow

Contents

1	A Strange Request	9
2	Ghostly Attack	18
3	Vanishing Clue	29
4	Accusations	38
5	Diamond Thief	49
6	The Mysterious Landslide	59
7	Shadow Canyon	68
8	Scotty's Castle	79
9	Vanished!	89
10	Kidnapped!	100
11	Fire	110
12	Old Friends	122
13	Horse Show Honours	130
14	Unexpected Wrangler	139
15	A Timely Trap	151

Chica came galloping around the rocks . . .

Glossary

Adobe Sun-dried bricks used for building in California, Mexico and Arizona.

Buckskin A horse that is greyish-yellow in colour—literally, the colour of a "buck" or male deer.

Burro Donkey.

Busboy A waiter's assistant.

Cookout A party where the food is cooked outside.

Corral A pen for cattle or horses.

Dude ranch A ranch used as a holiday resort offering facilities like riding and camping.

Faucet Tap.

Mesa Flat tableland with steep edges.

Pinto A horse marked with white patches—piebald or skewbald.

Quarter horse A small, powerful breed of horse, originally bred for sprinting in quarter-mile races in Virginia in the eighteenth century.

Saddlebred A type of horse bred for riding.

Saddlehorn The pommel of a western saddle round which a lasso can be looped.

Sidewalk Pavement.

A Strange Request 1

"Are you sure you and Doña won't be lonesome if Bob and I accept a Thanksgiving invitation?" Linda Craig asked her grandfather as they stood near the corral on Rancho del Sol. "Traditionally, it is a family holiday."

Tom "Bronco" Mallory smiled at his slim, sixteen-year-old granddaughter. "As a matter of fact, Doña and I have plans of our own. Some old friends are vacationing in California this month, so we'll be entertaining them. Suppose you tell me a little about the Rogerses." His blue eyes were kind, and Linda smiled, relieved of the twinges of guilt she'd felt ever since the invitation had arrived that morning.

Linda's Spanish colouring marked her as a proud descendant of an earlier Rosalinda for whom she'd been named. Her sandy-haired, eighteen-year-old brother Bob favoured their Scottish background. They had come to live with the Mallorys after their parents were killed in an accident, and a wonderful closeness had been formed.

"Uncle Biff and Aunt Elaine Rogers were friends of Mum and Dad," Linda explained. "We were stationed on the same army posts several times, so they used to call Bob and me their adopted niece and nephew." She giggled. "They don't have any children, so they used to borrow us to go to the circus or the zoo, things like that."

"They sound like very nice people," Bronco observed.

"They retired last year and went to Nevada, where they bought Shadow Canyon Guest Ranch. It's a dude ranch located not far from Death Valley." Linda's smile faded. "According to Aunt Elaine's letter, everything was going fine until just recently."

"What happened?"

"They have a ghost."

"A what?" Bronco sounded sceptical.

"They don't believe in ghosts either," Linda replied, "but something is making life miserable for them and their guests. They are really afraid that they will have to give up the ranch if they can't find out what's going on."

Bronco studied her for a moment. "They want you and Bob to help them catch their ghost, is that it?"

"And Kathy and Larry, too, if they can go with us," Linda answered, hoping to include her brother's and her best friends Kathy Hamilton and Larry Spencer in the promised adventure. "And we'll be close enough to explore Death Valley," she added. "Plus, Chica d'Oro has been invited."

"Chica, too?" Bronco was amused. "Has your horse added ghost hunting to her list of tricks?"

Linda laughed with him, then reached out to stroke the neck of Chica d'Oro, the beautiful palomino filly who'd come across the corral to nuzzle her shoulder as she talked. "Not exactly," the tall brunette admitted. "But there is a horse show being held on a ranch just outside Las Vegas, and Uncle Biff suggested I might enter Chica in the Parade Horse Class. What do you think?"

"It sounds like you will have a very busy

vacation," Bronco remarked, giving her a quick hug.

"You approve then?" Linda asked.

"If you and Bob want to help the Rogerses, I think you should. Why don't you go inside and call Kathy now?"

Linda grinned. "I'll have to wait till Bob finishes talking to Larry."

Bronco laughed. "Sounds to me like you were pretty sure of my approval."

"Doña was here when we got the letter and she said she knew you'd want us to go."

Bob emerged from the ranch house just as Linda reached it. "What did Larry say?" she asked.

"That he's always wanted to explore Death Valley and he'd love to spend the Thanksgiving holidays on a dude ranch." Then his tone became more serious as he asked, "Did Bronco give his permission?"

Linda nodded, her dark eyes sparkling with delight. "I'm on my way to call Kathy to see if she can go, too."

An hour later the teenagers' plans were completed. They were to leave early the next day to make the drive to the dude ranch.

Bob rubbed his freckled nose. "I'd better call Uncle Biff and Aunt Elaine," he said, "and tell them to expect four people and two horses sometime late tomorrow afternoon."

"It's too bad Patches has a stone bruise," Linda remarked, thinking about Kathy's pinto. "But I'm sure the Rogerses will have plenty of horses for Larry and Kathy to ride. Besides, it's easier to pull a two-horse trailer with just Rocket and Chica." Rocket was Bob's handsome bay quarter horse.

"I can hardly wait to get started," Bob said. "I've

read so much about Scotty's Castle, Devils Golf Course, and all the other places in Death Valley."

"Oh, you," Linda said, shaking her head. "We're supposed to be ghost hunting, remember? Death Valley is an extra-added attraction."

"Since I don't believe in ghosts, that's going to be easy," Bob prophesied. "We'll catch whoever is doing those things to the ranch's guests on the first day and then we'll be free to spend the rest of our vacation exploring."

"I hope you're right, Mr Ghost Catcher," Linda told him, "but Uncle Biff and Aunt Elaine seem awfully worried, and they don't believe in ghosts either, you know. They just haven't been able to find any clues to who or what is doing this to them and their guests."

"Maybe you can train Chica to stalk the ghost," Bob suggested, his eyes full of fun.

"Bronco already thought of that," Linda answered, "and it might not be such a bad idea. I'm sure she has more sense than some people."

"Horse sense," Bob teased, unbothered. "Anyway, she'll be there for the horse show and that's the important thing. She'll be competing with some pretty fine horses in the Las Vegas area."

"We'll look at the class listings," Linda said. "Maybe there are some you and Rocket can enter."

"Don't worry if there aren't," Bob said generously. "Larry, Kathy, and I will be happy to be your cheering section. You and Chica are the perfect team to represent Shadow Canyon Guest Ranch."

"Let's hope we're the right people to help Uncle Biff and Aunt Elaine," Linda replied. "They sounded so worried in their letter, Bob," she added with concern in her voice.

"I'll reassure them when I call," Bob said, whistling as he headed for the phone.

Linda went down to the corral where Chica d'Oro was standing, staring off towards the pasture where more of the ranch horses grazed.

"Hi, girl," she said, reaching out a hand to caress the filly's sleek golden hide. Linda smoothed the thick white mane neatly on one side of the animal's neck. Chica moved close to the rails, her brown eyes bright with curiosity.

Linda patted the horse again, then reached out a hand and stroked her shiny back. She was tempted to ride the filly bareback. After a moment's hesitation, she climbed on the corral fence and slid lightly onto Chica's back. The palomino looked at her questioningly, waiting for Linda to signal what she wanted her pet to do.

Linda pressed her thighs into the filly's sides, urging her forward. She placed one hand on each side of Chica d'Oro's neck, then leaned to the right. Chica responded properly, stepping diagonally across the corral. Linda bent farther to the right, turning the horse in a large circle, then leaned abruptly left, guiding her in a second circle to form a perfect figure eight.

"Chica, you're so smart," she praised the filly, relaxing her legs and resting back slightly so the palomino stopped. "I could ride you anywhere without a bridle or a saddle, couldn't I?"

Chica d'Oro nickered, then turned her head around and nuzzled Linda's knee affectionately, obviously agreeing with the idea. Linda dug in her pocket and produced a piece of carrot for the filly, then took her around the corral and back into the figure eight pattern in reverse. The horse responded flawlessly to the cues of Linda's legs and the shifting of her weight.

"I don't know how you do it, Sis," Bob called, coming to lean on the corral rail. "Chica almost seems able to read your mind."

"Sometimes I think she does," Linda agreed, riding over to the corral fence and sliding down to face her tall brother. "So what did Uncle Biff have to say?" she asked.

"Not much really," Bob admitted, his smile fading, "but he sure sounds upset, Linda. I think this ghost business is getting to him."

"They still want us to come, don't they?"

"They promise to welcome us with open arms."

It was dark the next morning when Linda and Bob loaded Chica d'Oro and Rocket into the trailer and drove off to pick up Kathy and Larry for the trip to Nevada. Kathy climbed into the car yawning, her honey blonde hair tousled. "When you said we'd leave early, I didn't realize you meant this unheard-of hour," she murmured, giggling.

"We've got a long drive and we want to get there before dinner," Bob explained.

"They want to look for the ghost in daylight," Larry contributed. He'd arrived late the evening before and spent the night at the Hamilton ranch to save time in the morning.

"Ghost?" Kathy sounded dubious. "You were joking about that, weren't you, Linda?"

Linda sighed. "I don't believe in ghosts, but

evidently some of the guests at the ranch do. They've been leaving in droves. In fact, if we can't find out who is playing ghost, the Rogerses may have to give up the dude ranch."

"But how can we possibly do that?" Kathy asked.

"Linda has secretly trained Chica to be a bloodhound and she's going to use her to track down the ghost," Bob teased.

"Better Chica than me," Kathy replied. "I'd just as soon not see it."

The trip proved to be uneventful, and it was still full daylight when Bob turned off the highway, crossed the cattle grid and followed the narrower road that marked the way to the Shadow Canyon Guest Ranch. The country was as rough and broken as much of the area around Rancho del Sol, but the road was a good one and they could see the handsome adobe buildings in the distance.

"Ready to meet the ghost?" Bob asked.

"How about just introducing us to the Rogerses?" Kathy suggested. "You can have the ghost."

"They must be waiting for us," Linda observed, peering ahead at several people standing together.

"I don't think so," Bob corrected as one of the figures left the other two and got into a battered old car. "More like they're saying goodbye to someone."

"Doesn't exactly look like a guest," Kathy said as the car passed them and they caught a quick glimpse of a middle-aged woman at the wheel.

"Guess we'll find out now," Bob said, pulling to a stop. "We're here!"

The welcome was warm, but once everyone had been introduced, Linda looked up at her hostess. "Aunt Elaine, is something wrong?" she asked.

Elaine Rogers sighed and pushed back the wind-tugged tendrils of her short auburn hair. "I'm sorry, Linda and Bob, I really meant for your welcome to be so happy. I mean we're delighted you're here, but . . . That was our cook leaving."

"Your cook!" Bob exclaimed.

Mr Rogers nodded, his blue eyes troubled. "I'm afraid you arrived just in time to see her leave us for good."

"Without having done a thing about tonight's dinner," his wife added.

"What happened?" Linda asked sympathetically.

"What else—the ghost scared her. She claims it has been stalking her for weeks. She heard some noise near the barn and . . ." Mrs Rogers paused for a moment. "It was probably just a cat or a mouse—but Cook's gone and she won't be back."

"Well, then I guess we'd better get busy," Linda said, straightening her shoulders. "If you'll show us where we'll be staying, the boys can unload the horses and we'll see what can be done about dinner."

"Dinner?" Aunt Elaine looked shocked. "I invited you here as guests, not to work."

"Do you have many guests to feed?" Bob asked.

"Fortunately, just three," Uncle Biff replied. "Mr David Pendleton, a widower, is here from Michigan with his two children. They're the only ones who haven't been scared away by our resident haunt."

"So it shouldn't be too difficult for us to fix something special, should it, Aunt Elaine?" Linda asked, a twinkle in her eye. "What did you have planned?"

The woman looked at Linda and her lips twitched into an embarrassed smile. Then she began to laugh. "Would you believe I haven't the slightest idea?" she asked. "You know me, Linda, cooking is not something I do well."

"Well, you're in luck tonight," Linda said, "because Bob, Kathy, Larry, and I are all very much at home in the kitchen, aren't we, gang?"

"Ah—" Bob looked a little doubtful and Kathy's nod was less than enthusiastic. Larry didn't even respond.

Linda surveyed the scene. "How about a cookout?" she suggested. "It's a nice day and that's something we've all had experience doing."

"Sounds fine to me," Uncle Biff told them, "and I'm sure the Pendletons would be in favour. We haven't done anything like that since they've been here."

"So let's get started!" Linda exclaimed.

"Larry and I will make Chica and Rocket comfortable," Bob told her. "You and Kathy can get the cookout organized."

"And make plans for the capture of our resident spook," Uncle Biff added. "If you four can't help us get rid of whatever is haunting this ranch all the cookouts in the world aren't going to do us any good."

Ghostly Attack 2

But before Linda could settle in, her brother called her outside. There, she was startled to see Chica standing about a hundred yards away, just looking at her. "Is this a joke?" Linda asked.

"She won't let us catch her," Bob answered. Even as they watched, Chica dodged away from Larry, loping a few strides, then looking back towards Linda.

"She's not running away," Linda told Bob. "She wants me to follow her."

"You can take Rocket," Bob offered. "Let me saddle him for you."

"You come, too," Linda suggested. "We can ride double."

In a few minutes they were both on the big bay and galloping after the golden filly, who raced away the instant they were mounted. Bob muttered angrily about chasing wild geese, but Linda said nothing, sure that Chica must have something more than a late-afternoon romp in mind.

As they rode, she became aware of the eerie rocks and deeply shadowed breaks that formed the ranch land. Everything seemed peaceful, but once they left the ranch buildings, her sharp ears caught another sound, a distant braying.

"There's a burro out here somewhere," she told Bob.

"I hear it," he admitted, slowing Rocket as Chica turned away from them and disappeared between two rough outcroppings of rock. Bob guided the bigger horse through the opening carefully, then stopped him.

A small, dun-coloured burro was braying noisily, the sound echoing in the rocky chamber. There was a second sound, too, a much weaker answering cry. Chica was standing close to the burro, whickering and nuzzling the unhappy beast as though trying to reassure her.

As they slid off Rocket, the burro turned towards them defensively, her big ears turned back, her teeth bared.

"Wait, Sis," Bob warned, his hand warm on her arm. "That's a wild burro."

"But there's something in that hole in the ground," Linda protested. "Something that needs help!"

"If you get kicked or bitten, you can't help it, whatever it is," Bob told her. "Maybe I could rope the burro and use Rocket to drag her away or . . ."

Chica, who'd appeared to be listening to the conversation, suddenly changed her tactics, moving firmly between the burro and Linda, nickering and squealing in a kind of warning conversation. Linda pulled free of Bob and hurried to look down over the edge of the small hole in the rocky floor: It was a baby burro!

The animal looked up at her with wide-eyed fear, trying to move away, but was trapped by the sides of the hole. Linda studied the situation for a moment, then carefully lowered herself over the side, dropping lightly to the ground beside the baby.

"Throw down your rope, Bob," she called, reaching out a slow, careful hand to the animal, crooning to it till it stopped trying to dodge away and surrendered, shivering, to her touch.

The burro was quite young and seemed unhurt except for several scrapes and bruises on his grey sides and on one slim leg. The rope dropped and Linda worked quickly, first fashioning it into a rough harness, then guiding the baby to the shallowest side of the hole.

"Pull slowly," she cautioned Bob, who was now mounted on Rocket, the other end of the rope secured around the saddle horn. "I'll get him started up, and with your help, I think he can make it out on his own feet."

For a moment, it appeared they might not be able to do it, for the little burro fought the harness instead of trying to climb, but a soft call from his mother changed his mind and he began to scramble up the loose shale of the incline. Without the pull of the rope as Rocket moved away from the hole, he would never have made it; but with that help, he was soon over the lip of the hole and safe.

"I'll get you out in a minute, Sis," Bob called as he hurried to free the little burro so he could run to his now-frantic mother.

Bob tossed Linda the rope and she climbed out as Rocket held it steady. She reached the top just in time to see the two burros racing out of the small canyon.

"Not even a thank you," Bob told her with a grin.

Linda laughed. "Seeing him safe and alive instead of starving to death in this hole is enough." She hurried over to Chica.

Bob nodded. "Chica must have heard the mother from the ranch," he commented. "She knew they needed help."

"So she brought us." Linda hugged Chica. "Wasn't she brave to keep the mother from attacking us? I'm surprised she didn't get kicked."

Bob chuckled. "The mother quit fussing the minute you dropped into the hole with her baby. I guess Chica convinced her that we were just trying to help."

Linda gave the filly a last pat, then vaulted onto her back. "Now I suppose we'd better get back and help with that cookout," she said. "It may not be as exciting as Chica's rescue, but it is necessary."

As it turned out, things were well underway by the time they reached the ranch house. There was little to do after they stabled the horses except to join the Pendletons and their friends around the campfire that Mr Rogers and Wayne Upton, the ranch hand, had built. While they ate, Linda and Bob told the story of Chica's rescue of the baby burro.

Sylvia, Mr Pendleton's thirteen-year-old daughter, and Jimmy, her ten-year-old brother, were very impressed. "She must be the smartest horse around," Sylvia said shyly.

"Well, she is a trick horse," Linda admitted, her pride in Chica's achievements overcoming her own modesty.

"Would you show us?" Jimmy asked.

"Not tonight," Linda answered, "but maybe tomorrow we could put on a little show for you."

Kathy, Larry, and Bob began to tell everyone about the trick shows that Linda and Chica had given and to describe the trophies and ribbons that she and the filly had won in horse shows. Embarrassed, Linda got to her feet, and excused herself, saying that she would go to the kitchen and check on the dessert.

Once away from the campfire, she slowed her steps. It was a lovely night, the sky bright with stars and not even a breeze stirring the bushes and trees that shaded the adobe-style buildings of the ranch. All it lacked was guests, and that was the fault of the ghost. She sighed, her mind returning to the original reason for their visit.

A plaintive whinny came from the barn, and Linda turned her steps in that direction, knowing that it was Chica calling for company. It was very dark inside the barn, but the door was open, so Linda slipped inside.

"What's the matter, girl?" she asked. "Are you feeling lonesome in a strange stall?"

Chica's velvety nostrils rubbed against Linda's cheek and she put her arms around the filly's warm neck. "I'm sorry you couldn't come to the campfire," she told her, "but—"

Linda stopped as a sound reached her ears. Something was moving on the other side of the barn. Rocket? Another head reached out to her and she remembered that the two Old Sol horses had been stabled side-by-side.

The sound continued, a shuffling noise like someone dragging something along the dirt floor of the barn. "Who . . . who's there?" Linda inquired, trying hard to keep her nervousness from showing in her voice.

The shuffling stopped for a moment, then began again, this time moving in her direction. Chica was no longer nuzzling her, and when she touched the filly's neck, Linda could feel the tension in it and she knew that Chica was listening, too.

Suddenly the sounds became more menacing, and Linda could make out a faintly luminous glow. Chica d'Oro snorted and dodged back, her hooves banging against the sides of the stall. Linda tried to reach out to calm her, but before she could, something crashed into her and sent her sprawling on the hard ground.

Cloth whispered over her face like the touch of cobwebs. As she tried to move away from her attacker, she was conscious again of the luminous glow. This time it was heading away from her into the darker shadows of the barn's interior.

Chica's squeal of fury came from above her, and Linda shuddered as steel-shod hooves crashed into the stall door beside her. "Chica, Chica, it's all right," she called, scrambling to her feet to comfort the horse even before she brushed the dirt and straw from her clothes and skin.

"Take it easy, girl, I'm all right," she continued, her fingers finding Chica's mane and catching it to pull the filly's head around to her. "Everything is going to be fine." She tried to sound confident, but her hands were shaking as she petted the palomino.

"Linda, are you in here?" Bob's voice came from outside the barn, giving his sister a deep sense of relief.

"I'm with Chica," she called.

"What's going on?" Larry asked.

"Are you all right?" Kathy inquired. "We came to look for you."

"We heard Chica," Bob explained, and Linda could see the outlines of the three of them in the

The horse reared in terror . . .

barn's open door. "What's going on?"

"Can you get some light?" she asked. "Something just happened."

"There are flashlights in the trailer," Bob said. "I'll get them."

In a moment two welcome beams of light appeared, and the three came into the barn. Linda blinked as one beam raked over her. "What in the world happened to you?" Bob asked, frowning.

"I think I've just met the ghost," Linda answered.

"The ghost!" Kathy looked around nervously. "Where?"

"I heard Chica whinny and I came in to talk to her for a minute," Linda explained. "Then I heard this funny noise coming from over there." As she pointed across the barn, both boys turned the flashlights in that direction.

"I don't see anything," Larry said. "What did it sound like?"

"A shuffling noise, like someone limping or maybe dragging something." Linda gave Chica a final pat and went over to look at the ground on the far side.

"There's nothing over here," she admitted, after kicking a little at the old straw that covered most of the dirt floor.

"So then what happened?" asked Bob.

"I called out and asked who was there and it started coming towards me. That's when I saw a sort of glow."

"A glow?" Larry asked, doubt in his voice.

Linda nodded emphatically. "No definite figure, just a kind of luminous shape. Anyway, Chica saw it, too, because she got upset and dodged away.

That's when whatever it was hit me and knocked me down."

"It hit you?" Kathy looked like she was ready to run from the barn at the very thought.

"I fell down and something brushed over me. I tried to move away and I could see it heading towards the back of the barn. Chica became very excited. I thought she was going to kick the stall down."

"We heard her," Larry admitted, heading down the line of stalls towards the rear of the barn. "You say it went this way?" he asked, stopping to shine the flashlight into each stall.

"It sure did," Linda answered as she followed him with Bob and Kathy in her wake.

"Well, it doesn't appear to be here now," Larry announced, stopping at the last stall.

Bob lifted his light and checked the rafters, then went to look in each stall again. He returned, shaking his head. "There isn't even a loft in this barn, Linda, and there's no way out except the door we entered."

"No one came out that way," Kathy said. "We would have seen them if they had."

"Someone knocked me down," Linda protested.

"Or some*thing*," Kathy murmured.

"I don't believe in ghosts," Linda stated firmly. "May I have a torch please?"

"Be my guest," Larry said, handing one to her. "But if there was anyone hiding in any of the stalls, we would have seen him."

Linda marched back to Chica's stall and tried to place herself exactly where she'd been earlier. Then she turned the light in the direction the sound and shape had gone. The beam moved down the open aisle between the stalls and ended at the patched and untidy rear wall of the barn. There simply wasn't anything unusual or out of place.

"Maybe there really is a ghost," Bob said, his tone telling her that he was only half-teasing.

Linda didn't answer as she walked slowly along the aisle, the beam of the torch shining on the hard-packed earth. About halfway down the row of stalls, she stopped.

"Find something?" Larry asked, hurrying to stand beside her.

"It looks like a boot print," Linda said, indicating the faint indentation in the dusty earth.

"It could be one of ours," Bob commented, joining them.

"Your feet aren't that big," Linda told him.

"How about Uncle Biff's or Mr Upton's?" Larry suggested.

Linda shrugged, then continued along the aisle. "Here's another one," she announced, stopping at once. "And it's much clearer. See the notch there in the side of the sole—there's some kind of design on the boot heel, too. Notice how the imprint is smudged there in the middle?"

Bob knelt down beside her. "You're right about that, Sis," he agreed. "That is really a distinctive boot print. We should be able to tell right away if it came from Mr Pendleton, or Mr Upton, or Uncle Biff."

Linda nodded, but she was already moving on along the aisle, seeking more clues. The hard ground yielded little else, however, till she was almost to the rear wall. There, next to the panels and boards that had been used to repair the battered and broken original wood, was a slightly damp spot and in it was a perfect boot print.

"Over here," she called.

"It's a clover leaf," Kathy said, peering at the heel print. "That's on the heel."

"And the notch is right there on the inside of the left boot," Linda pointed out.

"Your ghost has big feet," Bob commented.

"A ghost that wears cowboy boots," Larry said. "That has got to be a first."

Linda grinned at them. "I told you there was someone in here," she said.

"But who?" Bob asked. "Everyone but you was at the campfire."

Linda frowned. "Everyone was there?"

The other three exchanged glances, then nodded. "Then it couldn't have been one of them," Linda mused.

"Well, at least this proves that your ghost is human," Bob said. "That should make Uncle Biff and Aunt Elaine happy."

Linda got to her feet and stepped back, looking around.

"What is it, Linda?" Kathy asked.

"If my ghost is human, where did he go?" Linda asked. "And why in the world would he leave a boot print there?"

The others stared at her for a moment, then looked back at the boot print, suddenly seeing what Linda had just noticed. The clear boot print was less than a foot from the wall and facing directly towards solid boards!

Vanishing Clue 3

No one said anything for several moments. Then Kathy sighed. "What are we going to do?" she asked.

Bob looked at Linda. "I think we'd better get back to the campfire," he said. "People are going to wonder where we are."

Linda nodded. "You three go ahead," she suggested. "I've got to wash off some of this grime."

"Why don't I go with you, Linda," Kathy said. "That way we can take the dessert down to the others and no one will wonder why we were gone so long."

"Aren't you going to tell them what happened?" Larry asked, surprised.

"I'll tell Uncle Biff and Aunt Elaine," Linda answered, "but I'm sure they wouldn't want us to worry the Pendletons about it."

"We can just say we checked on Chica because she was whinnying," Bob suggested. "That would be the truth anyway."

"And we can look at everyone's boots," Larry added, "to see if any has a clover-leaf heel."

Linda gave Chica a final consoling pat. She disliked leaving the filly alone in the barn, since she had no idea where the intruder had gone, but she seemed to have no choice at the moment.

Once in the kitchen, she washed, then combed the

bits of straw from her hair while Kathy got things ready to take to the campfire. Bob arrived just as they were trying to decide how they could carry everything down to the group in one trip.

"Need some help?" he asked.

"Do we," Linda agreed. "I'd forgotten that we'll need the coffee and hot chocolate as well as the dessert."

"Did anyone ask about us?" Kathy inquired.

Bob shook his head. "They were all busy planning for tomorrow. They're going to take a picnic and ride to Shadow Canyon. Doesn't that sound like fun?"

"Are we invited?" Linda asked.

"Of course. Everyone is eager to show us around." Bob grinned at her. "I think they want to see what adventures Chica will find on the trail."

Linda laughed. "Just so she doesn't find any ghosts."

The rest of the evening proved pleasant. They finished the food, then sat around the dying fire and sang a mixture of popular and western songs. Biff Rogers had a strong, true voice that carried the rest of them easily, and Aunt Elaine remembered most of the words, which helped.

Jimmy was half-asleep by the time the fire had become glowing embers and the night wind had risen cold and eerie in the trees. Since the wrangler Upton had disappeared shortly after the food, Bob and Larry helped Uncle Biff bury the embers, then carried the grills to the kitchen where they were put to soak till morning.

"I'll call an employment agency tomorrow and see if they can find a cook for us," Aunt Elaine promised as she cleaned up the kitchen. "I can handle breakfast and a picnic lunch, so there's only dinner to worry about."

She sounded so calm and happy Linda felt a twinge of guilt as she said, "I'm afraid there is something else, Aunt Elaine."

"What's that?" Mrs Rogers asked, her green eyes instantly wary. "Did you find something out there besides a baby burro that needed to be rescued from a hole?"

Linda nodded, then gave her an accurate report on everything that had occurred in the barn and what they'd found afterwards.

Uncle Biff listened intently, a frown drawing his dark eyebrows into a single heavy line over his eyes. "Why didn't you say something before?" he asked when she finished. "Maybe we could have caught whoever it was."

Bob shook his head. "There wasn't anybody around the barn. Larry and I checked every nook and cranny before we headed back to the fire. And nobody left there either; because we would have seen them while we were walking back."

Mr Rogers sighed. "Are you trying to tell me there really is a ghost?" he demanded, his tone harsh with frustration.

"Of course not," Linda answered. "We just didn't think it would do any good to upset the Pendletons, since whoever it was had already disappeared."

"You're probably right about that," Aunt Elaine admitted. "If we lose them, I don't know what we will do. We have some bookings for the Christmas holidays, but if we can't find out what or who is doing this to us . . ." Her voice broke.

"We'll solve the mystery, I'm sure," Linda said with what she hoped was more confidence than she felt at the moment. "Bob and I will make a cast of the boot print in the morning and then all we'll have to do is find the wearer of the boots!"

"Someone who can walk through walls," Kathy added, dampening everyone's enthusiasm. They quickly dispersed to their rooms.

"Did you mean what you told them, Linda?" Kathy asked once she was in bed. "I mean about finding their ghost."

"I'm going to do my best," Linda answered.

"You think it's a person, don't you?"

Linda nodded. "I've never heard of a ghost wearing cowboy boots and, anyway, Chica was angry, not frightened. She wanted to go after whatever it was."

"She'd have run into a blank wall," Kathy reminded her.

"What's on the other side of the wall, do you know?" Linda asked.

"Bob said that there is a big pile of hay bales outside." Kathy frowned. "Why?"

Linda shrugged. "I thought maybe there was a sliding panel or something, but no one would be going through a wall and into a bale of hay."

Kathy giggled, and, after a moment, Linda joined in. "I guess we'll figure it out tomorrow," Linda said, closing her eyes and trying to relax into sleep.

Morning came with a crash and clatter from the direction of the kitchen. Linda sat up and looked around wildly for a moment, then remembered where she was. Kathy yawned at her, her apricot-tinted complexion rosy with sleep. "Sounds like our hostess is taking care of breakfast," she observed with a smile.

"We'd better help her while there are still enough dishes left to serve the meal," Linda replied, giggling. "Aunt Elaine is a terrific lady and more fun than anybody around, but the kitchen is not her favourite place."

"The Rogerses are great," Kathy said. "I'm glad we came."

"Me, too."

Once dressed, the girls hurried through the big dining room and into the warm, busy kitchen. "About time you got here," Larry called from the sink, where he had just finished washing the grills.

"Good morning," Aunt Elaine greeted them from the stove. "Do you still remember how to make pancakes, Linda?"

"She's improved," Bob answered for her.

"I can even flip them without missing the pan," Linda agreed, pleasantly reminded of the years they'd lived near the Rogerses.

Breakfast preparations went quickly, and by the time Mr Upton and the Pendletons arrived in the dining room, there was nothing to do except pour coffee, milk, and orange juice, and serve the food. Mr Pendleton was the first to sample the pancakes and he smiled across the table at Linda. "Somebody is a better cook than the one who left," he complimented her.

"That's what I told them last night," Uncle Biff agreed. "I just wish we could hire the four of them permanently."

Everyone laughed and the conversation turned easily to the ride they were to make that morning.

"We should probably turn Chica and Rocket out in the corral for a little while before we saddle up," Linda commented when she'd eaten her fill of the pancakes, scrambled eggs and sausage. "They might be a little stiff from the long ride in the trailer yesterday."

Bob's eyes met hers in quick understanding. "I'll go right out," he said.

"Why don't you join him, Linda," Aunt Elaine suggested.

Kathy nodded. "Larry and I will help with the dishes and fix the lunch."

In a few minutes, Linda and Bob were hurrying towards the barn to make a cast of the boot print they'd found the night before. However, before they reached the open door, there was a rush of footsteps behind them and Sylvia and Jimmy came running up.

Bob met Linda's gaze, then suggested, "Hey, Sis, why don't you limber Chica up by running her through some of her tricks for Sylvia and Jimmy?"

"Oh, would you?" Sylvia's eyes danced.

"We'd love to," Linda assured her. Though she would have preferred helping make the cast, this did seem a perfect solution to the problem of keeping everyone away while Bob did the task.

Chica d'Oro moved forward quickly when Linda opened her stall, but her gait was uneven. Linda stopped her at once and she and Bob bent to examine her slender legs and delicate pasterns. It took only a moment to detect the slight swelling in her right hind fetlock.

"It just looks like a slight strain," Bob said, "from the ride or maybe from kicking the stall."

"What's the matter?" Sylvia asked.

"Chica's just a little lame," Linda answered, leading Rocket and the filly out to the corral so Bob could be alone in the barn.

"What are you going to do?" Jimmy asked.

"Just let her rest her leg for a day or so," Linda answered as she entered the corral with the two horses. "Do you think that's a good idea, Chica?"

The filly looked at her, then nodded her head up and down in response to Linda's cue.

"Does your leg hurt a lot?" Linda asked.

Chica shook her head in a vigorous no.

"Are you sorry you can't go on the ride?"

Again the golden head nodded, the small ears pricked forward alertly.

Jimmy and Sylvia shouted with delight and clapped as Linda gave Chica the signal to bow to them. Linda rewarded her with several bites of an apple she'd brought from the kitchen, then gave Rocket a bite as he came over to investigate.

"Does she do more tricks?" Jimmy asked as Linda stood stroking the filly's neck.

"She's learning more all the time," Linda answered, "but some of them would put a strain on her sore leg, so we'll have to wait till later to do them."

"Is it hard to teach Chica things?" Sylvia questioned.

"Oh, no," Linda replied. "She loves to perform, so she's always willing to learn something new."

"A smart horse like that must be worth a lot of money," another voice said, and Linda looked up to see Wayne Upton, the Rogerses' tall, lean wrangler, standing at the rail. "'Specially when she's a fancy colour, too."

"Chica is not for sale," Linda informed him coolly.

"Are the horses ready for the ride?" Sylvia asked the wrangler.

"We have a problem," Upton answered, his tone making it plain that it was nothing that bothered *him*.

"What's wrong?" Linda asked at once.

"Somebody left the corral gate latch loose and the horses got out. I've caught four of them, but the rest are scattered over the hills." He shrugged. "They can't go too far, but with all the canyons, they're hard to find. We usually just leave the gate open and they wander in when they get hungry."

"Did you catch Poco?" Sylvia asked worriedly.

Upton nodded. "Caught him and the pinto and a couple of others that were close to the barn, so your family is set for the ride." His gaze turned to Linda. "I don't know about horses for your friends. Maybe you could go round up a couple more, if you really want to go on this ride." His tone was heavy with lack of invitation.

"I think maybe we should just skip this ride." Bob spoke from behind her, making both Linda and Chica start nervously. "Chica is lame and it won't hurt Rocket to have a day off after that long ride in the trailer."

Linda turned to look at her brother, sensing that there was more behind his words than just a desire to miss the ride into the hills. After a moment she turned back to the wrangler. "Are you sure the horses will be all right?" she asked.

"When nobody is riding them, they run loose. The ranch property is fenced," Upton answered over his shoulder as he walked away, heading around the barn to the corral on the far side where the ranch horses had been kept. Sylvia and Jimmy hesitated for a moment, then followed him, leaving Linda alone with her brother.

"Sure makes you feel wanted, doesn't he?" Linda observed, then asked, "Did you make the cast already?"

"I couldn't," Bob answered.

"What do you mean?" Linda frowned at him.

"Go see for yourself," Bob advised, then followed her into the barn.

It was quiet inside with the horses still out in the corral, and Linda moved confidently along the aisle, which was now well lit by the sunshine that streamed in through two windows and the open door. Only the back of the barn was dim, but Bob had picked up a torch, which he handed to her without a word.

Linda turned it on as she crossed to the exact spot along the wall where she'd found the boot print the night before. The light shone down clearly, picking up the neat grooves of a well-raked floor. The boot print had vanished!

Accusations 4

"We seem to have a very neat ghost," Bob said, frustration showing in his tone.

"But who . . . Why . . .?"

"Maybe he overheard us last night," Bob suggested.

Linda sighed. "Well, I'm just glad that the rest of you saw that boot print, too, or I'd probably think I was crazy."

"So what now?" Bob asked.

"I guess we'd better go up to the house and tell everybody about the ranch horses being gone," Linda replied. "And about Chica's being lame."

"First I want to check the other side of this wall," Bob said. "Maybe we'll find a clue."

Linda followed him around the barn. The end of the building was a blank wall, but a small lean-to roof had been attached to it to shelter the large stacks of hay bales that were piled beside the wall. Linda slowly circled the bales, her eyes on the ground; but there was nothing to be seen.

"Looks like this is where the horses spent a part of their time," Bob said, pointing to the variety of hoofprints that surrounded the wire fence around the hay.

"I wonder why the horses would run away," Linda mused, looking out at the rather barren landscape of the ranch. "Most times when horses get out, they just hang around close and wait for someone to come and feed them."

"Maybe something scared them," Bob suggested. "Larry and I heard coyotes last night, so they could have spooked them."

"I suppose so," Linda agreed. "Well, let's go give Kathy and Larry the bad news about the ride."

Uncle Biff frowned when Bob told them about the loose horses. "That's the second time this month that has happened," he said. "I think we're going to have to get a new catch for the corral gate."

"You're welcome to use Rocket to round up your horses," Bob told him. "With Chica lame, we won't be going on the ride anyway."

The rancher shook his head. "They should all be here by afternoon. Since they're gone, they've missed their morning oats, so they'll be home for dinner. All I have to do is close the gate."

Aunt Elaine sighed. "Well, if you can't go riding, why don't the four of you go over to Death Valley? I'll call the Furnace Creek Inn and make arrangements for you to have lunch there as my guests. It's the least I can do to repay you for all your hard work last night and this morning."

"That's not necessary," they all chorused.

"We insist," Uncle Biff said. "You'll love the place and it's on the drive from here to Scotty's Castle."

"Sounds great," Bob admitted. "I'm dying to see Death Valley. I've read so much about it."

"I just wish I didn't have to leave Chica," Linda murmured.

"Don't worry about her," Aunt Elaine said. "I'll be home all day and I can see the corral from here. I'll keep an eye on her for you."

"And I will, too," Uncle Biff promised. "I'll be watching for my horses all day." He shook his head. "If Wayne hadn't come so highly recommended, I'd wonder about him."

"He's very good with the guests," Aunt Elaine reminded him.

Uncle Biff sighed. "That's the important thing, I guess."

"If we're not going riding, we'd better change," Kathy told Linda.

"And I'd better get the map and find out where we're going," Bob added.

"Just be sure to wear sturdy shoes or boots," Aunt Elaine called after them. "The ground out there is rough and you'll want to do some exploring."

As they changed, Kathy looked at Linda, then down at herself, and laughed. "We're going to be pretty easy to spot in a crowd," she observed.

Linda, who'd been preoccupied wondering about the vanishing boot print, glanced at her friend, then joined in her laughter. Her well-cut western suit was a deep burgundy that went well with her dark hair and eyes and olive-toned complexion, while Kathy's kelly-green suit was perfect with her fair skin and golden colouring.

"Oh, well, we didn't want to be ignored," she replied. Still laughing, they went out to join Larry and Bob, who were just folding up the map.

"Ready to go?" Larry asked, his glance appreciative as he smiled at Linda.

"Your reservations are made," Aunt Elaine told them. "They only serve from noon till one p.m. so be sure to get there in time."

"We'll drive right along," Bob assured her. "And thank you."

"Have fun and don't worry about a thing," Uncle Biff called after them.

As they got in the car, four riders came around the barn, and Sylvia, Jimmy, and Mr Pendleton waved enthusiastically. Wayne Upton looked their way, then deliberately reined his horse away from the road.

"What did we do to him?" Larry asked, staring after the wrangler.

Bob shrugged. "I asked him if he'd raked the barn and he said it wasn't his job. Other than that, I haven't talked to him except at dinner or breakfast."

"So where do we go?" Linda changed the subject.

"And what do we see?" Kathy asked.

"Well," Bob answered, "we follow this road and before lunch there's just one stop. Zabriskie Point. It's on our way."

The drive was a pleasant one, but even before the signs told them they were in Death Valley, the eerie landscape told them they were there. Though they were used to desert, this was far beyond that. Naked rock rose in jagged folds. The colours changed constantly, some formations pale and grey or beige, others mustard gold or red.

Bob found the turnoff to Zabriskie Point and parked so they had a view of the strangely wrinkled land beyond. A single sharp headland rose from the rest to give the view its name, but the mysterious emptiness of the land beyond the badlands drew their eyes.

"Those are the Funeral Mountains," Bob said, pointing to the brooding range.

"Those are the Funeral Mountains," Bob said

"Thanks a lot," Kathy murmured, shivering though the air around them was warm.

"And those across the valley must be the Panamints," Larry commented, pointing to the distant range that rose to greet the sunlit sky.

"It's certainly a frightening-looking place," Linda observed. "Can you imagine trying to cross this area without a road . . . and in a wagon?"

"I don't see how anyone had the courage." Kathy sounded awe-struck.

"Well, I think I'll be more interested in the scenery after lunch," Bob told them, checking his watch. "I think we'd better keep moving if we're going to get to Furnace Creek Inn for lunch."

"I'm starving," Linda admitted.

"Me, too," the others chorused as they got into the car.

Each turn of the road brought new views that kept them gasping. Still, none of them was prepared for the shock of seeing trees and green grass growing right in the middle of the wasted paleness of the flat land.

"What is that?" Linda gasped, pointing.

"Is it a mirage?" Kathy asked.

"Unless this map is way off, that's the Furnace Creek Inn and Ranch Resort," Bob answered. "Your basic oasis in the desert."

"I don't believe it," Larry murmured.

"According to Uncle Biff, that part over there is the Ranch with the golf course and the date palm orchard." Bob waved his hand towards the left. "The one higher up is the Inn. That's where we're supposed to eat."

"It's beautiful," Linda whispered.

The road turned and headed up a steep hill to a small parking area in front of the Spanish-style villa that sat on a mesa above the desert floor. A fountain splashed in front of the rock wall of the building, and two rock staircases rose on each side of it to the main entrance of the Inn.

"Ready?" Bob asked, getting out.

"I can hardly wait," Linda answered.

The hallway was gracious, and as they approached the desk an older woman came from their right. She wore a small badge and a welcoming smile as she stopped in front of them. "Are you the guests from Shadow Canyon Ranch?" she asked.

They nodded, not surprised by the question.

"Elaine called and asked me to reserve a table for you," the woman continued. "This way, please." She led them into the spacious dining room and seated them at a table that overlooked the awesome view of both valley and the oasis of the Ranch resort below.

Ordering from the inviting menu occupied several minutes, and then they were free to look around as they waited for their lunch. Linda noticed that one of the young men who was helping the black-clad waitresses was watching their table with more than normal interest.

Was he admiring her or Kathy? Linda smiled in his direction, but there was no response, and after a moment, she realized that his gaze was directed at Bob. Curious, she touched her brother's arm.

"There's someone over by the fireplace who's watching you," she told him in a whisper. "The busboy with the red hair."

Bob sipped his water as he casually looked towards the fireplace that dominated one wall. Then his expression changed to one of delight. "That's Andy," he gasped. "Andy Greer, don't you remember him, Sis?"

Linda frowned, then laughed. "I didn't recognize him. We knew him when we were in school back East. He was sort of a big brother to Bob when we first entered that school."

Bob started to rise, then sank back as the stocky redhead gestured him to wait. "Maybe he isn't allowed to talk to guests," Larry suggested, looking around. "This place is pretty formal."

"I wonder what time he finishes," Bob murmured, regretfully turning his attention to the food that was being set before him.

Within a few moments the answer arrived in a note delivered by the busboy serving their table. He dropped it casually into Bob's lap, then winked. "Regulations," he whispered.

"MEET YOU BY THE POOL AS SOON AFTER 1.30 AS I CAN," the note read, and was signed "A".

"You didn't know he was working here?" Kathy asked as they began to eat.

Bob shook his head. "Andy and I write about four times a year and I think he owes me a letter. He's been having a tough time making it through college. He goes for a while, and then he has to take time off to work to pay his tuition and expenses."

"That must be why he's here," Linda observed. "Working and saving for next year."

"It's great to see him," Bob said. "We'll have to find out what days he's off so we can ask him over to the ranch. I'm sure Uncle Biff and Aunt Elaine won't mind another rider for a day."

"Maybe he can tell us some places to go in Death Valley, too," Larry suggested.

"I just wish he was assigned to this side of the room," Bob grumbled. "There's so much we've got to talk about."

"It's probably just as well he isn't," Linda teased. "You'd get him fired."

Bob laughed, then nodded his agreement to her assessment. "He's just a great guy. He really helped me. That was my first year in high school, and I didn't know anybody or anything that was going on."

"Hasn't changed much, has he?" Larry teased, winking at Linda.

"Not a bit," she agreed, then devoted her full attention to her lunch, enjoying it.

It was well after one when they finished, and the room was starting to empty. Bob looked around, but Andy was nowhere in sight, so they made their way out to the lobby.

Bob stopped to ask directions to the pool, then led the way outside. "I was told we can take any of the stairways that lead down, but since Andy will be tied up for a while, we might as well go that way and explore a little."

The Inn was a maze of two-storey buildings that wound up and down the hillside on which it was built. The style was Spanish, but most of the walkways and stairs were built in beautiful stonework.

Following instructions, they went through an archway and emerged on a walk above what appeared to be a garden. A tiny stream splashed and sparkled over a series of small waterfalls, pausing in deep, cooling ponds, then dropping again. Palms shaded the area and grass grew enthusiastically and lushly all about the rocky pathways that meandered through the area.

"Oh, let's go down that way," Kathy suggested. The others nodded their agreement, following her down the rock stairs to the narrow path that crossed and recrossed the little stream.

Since the area of garden was small, it didn't take long for them to explore it all and they were soon heading towards the inviting blue expanse of the pool. Here, too, they found more of the beautiful rock walls, this time forming a series of arches on one side of the pool, while the other side was protected by the building.

"Oh, I wish we could go in," Linda groaned as several people dived into the water. "It looks heavenly."

"After all the lunch we ate, we'd end up sinking to the bottom and not coming up," Larry warned.

"There's Andy!" Bob exclaimed and pointed towards another set of stairs that came more directly from the main building at the top of the hill.

Linda, Kathy, and Larry stayed at the poolside while Bob alone made his way between the tables with their bright umbrellas. Once the two stopped pounding each other on the back, Bob brought Andy over to join them.

"So how do you happen to be working here?" Linda asked once introductions were finished.

"By accident," Andy answered, grinning. "I started working at the Grand Canyon right after college ended last spring and I was offered a job down here for the winter, so I decided to stay out of school till summer session. I figure I should be able to save enough here to carry me through the whole year, next year. I might even be able to stretch it far enough to graduate."

"Hey, that's super," Linda told him. "Do you like it here?"

"It's not bad," Andy answered. "They're a little strict, but that's because it's a nice place and the guests expect the service to be top-notch."

"So when is your day off?" Bob asked.

"Well, I . . ."

"There he is!" A woman's voice carried above the noise of the swimmers and sunbathers.

Linda turned around and saw that the woman was coming their way and was followed by the man from the hotel desk. An icy fist of fear clutched in her stomach as the woman pointed at Bob and Andy.

"He's the one," she sobbed. "That's the boy who stole my diamonds!"

Diamond Thief 5

Bob and Andy whirled to face the woman and her angry-looking escort, both boys obviously too shocked by the accusation to speak. Linda, shaken herself, stepped forward. "Is . . . is something wrong?" she asked, her voice just a little uncertain.

The woman turned to glare at her. "That boy took my diamonds," she snapped, pointing to Andy. "I went for a walk before lunch and I saw him out in front of my room. He was pretending to work on the brush there, but he was probably watching me, waiting for a chance to get my diamonds." Her voice broke and she began to sob again.

"Now, Mrs Barker," the man began.

"You're his boss, Mr O'Roarke," the woman sobbed. "Make him give them back. Those diamonds are all I have and I want them back right now!"

"I didn't take your diamonds, Mrs Barker," Andy spoke up. "I was outside your room. That's part of my job. I keep the plants from growing over the wall and I sweep up the dust and leaves every morning."

"Did you see Mrs Barker leave her room, Andy?" Linda asked after waiting to see if the man was going to ask any questions.

Andy nodded, his blue eyes now turned her way imploringly. "I saw her leave, and then I went around the corner. I finished sweeping and headed back to wash and change for lunch." He paused, then added, "I was in the dining room when you came in, Mrs Barker."

The woman's fury melted and she wavered on her feet. Linda, fearful that she might faint, took her arm and gently guided her to a chair in the shade of one of the umbrella tables. "You're sure that the diamonds are gone?" she asked softly. "They couldn't just be mislaid?"

Dark eyes turned her way with contempt. "My dear young lady, I don't mislay a small fortune in diamonds, I can assure you."

Linda could feel the blaze of red in her cheeks, but she controlled the angry retort the woman deserved. After all, she thought wryly, the woman *had* left the diamonds in her room without any protection!

"When was the last time you saw your diamonds?" she asked. "And just what is missing?"

For a moment Mrs Barker looked as though she might not answer, but then she shrugged slightly. "A necklace, bracelet, and earrings," she replied. "All fine stones. They were a gift from my late husband."

Mr O'Roarke nodded, seeming to recover at last. "A lovely set," he agreed, "but not the sort of thing to be left unattended in your room, Mrs Barker."

The words were not spoken harshly, but the woman reacted as though slapped. "Is that all you can say?" she demanded. "Your employee steals my diamonds and you make it sound as though it's my fault. What kind of place is this?"

"I didn't take your diamonds," Andy protested. "I was never in your room."

"Humph." Mrs Barker's snort made it plain that she didn't believe him.

"You said that you went for a walk before lunch," Linda began, trying hard to divert the woman. "Did you see anyone else in the area?"

Mrs Barker started to speak, then seemed to reconsider and said nothing for several minutes. "There was a man on the hill behind the resort," she said at last, "but he was just looking at the view. He wouldn't know about my diamonds." She returned her glare to Andy. "He would."

Andy bristled, his bright hair like a flame in the desert sun. "If you think I took your diamonds, why don't you search me?" he demanded.

"I think perhaps we should go and check your room first, Mrs Barker," Mr O'Roarke said, looking around rather nervously. Linda was instantly aware of all the curious faces turned their way.

"If you think you're going to find my diamonds there, you're sadly mistaken," Mrs Barker grumbled, but she allowed herself to be escorted from the pool area.

"Please come with me," Andy said, looking at Bob and Linda.

"Of course we will," Bob answered, and the four young people followed the unfortunate redhead as they climbed to the long wing of the resort that rose above the garden area.

Mrs Barker's room was rather of a shambles when she led them inside. "Did the thief do this?" Mr O'Roarke asked, looking around.

Mrs Barker winced. "I did it," she admitted. "I was looking for my diamonds. I knew I'd left them in their box hidden in the dresser drawer, but when they weren't there . . ." She let it trail off, then turned to glare at Andy. "He probably peeked through the window and watched me hide them."

"I didn't take your diamonds," Andy protested once again.

"I think perhaps we should have a thorough search made," Mr O'Roarke said. "I'll call in the authorities."

Linda looked around the room, realizing there was little they could do here. "Could you show us where the man was, Mrs Barker?" she asked, eager to divert attention from Andy.

"I could," Andy offered. "I remember now, I saw him, too. He was starting back down the hill while I was finishing my sweeping."

"Was he a guest of the resort?" Mr O'Roarke asked at once, his attention diverted from his phone call.

Andy considered, then shook his head. "I don't think so. I didn't see his face clearly, because of his hat, but he had a beaky nose that I would have remembered. He was probably just a tourist."

"Suppose we go out there and take a look," Mr O'Roarke suggested, hanging up the phone. "It will be a while before the Sheriff gets here."

The hillside behind the resort buildings was a stark contrast to the rich garden area below. Andy pointed out the small ledge where the man had been standing.

Leaving Andy with Mrs Barker and Mr O'Roarke, Bob, Linda, Larry, and Kathy started up the rugged path to the ledge. "Andy couldn't have done it," Bob muttered as they climbed. "I just know that he couldn't."

"Of course he didn't," Linda agreed, her eyes on the ground under their feet. It was rough and shifting, but as they neared the ledge there was a single soft spot. "Wait!" she cried, stopping Bob just before he put his foot on the dusty earth.

"What is it?" Bob asked, startled.

"Look." Linda pointed at the boot print in the soil.

Bob glanced at it, then bent down to examine it with her. "That's it," he said. "It's got to be. The notch is there and the clover leaf in the heel and . . ."

"You mean the ghost was here?" Kathy asked as she and Larry joined them in examining the print.

"It sure looks like it," Linda answered.

"It's the same," Bob said, then moved on towards the ledge, watching the path more carefully now.

Linda followed him and they looked out over the resort and the valley. "It's a terrific view," Linda said, "but why would our ghost be interested in standing up here and looking out over the resort?"

"He could see anyone on the walkway from here," Larry observed.

"And Mrs Barker leaving her room," Linda suggested.

"Do you suppose he knew about the diamonds and was watching to see if she had them with her?" Bob asked.

Linda shrugged. "He should be as much of a suspect as Andy," she answered. "More, if we can make people believe that he was our ghost at the ranch."

"How can we expect anyone to believe that?" Larry asked. "I mean, we're the only ones who saw the boot print in the barn and now it's gone, so—"

"So they'll probably just think we're trying to help Andy," Bob finished for him.

"At least we can tell the Sheriff," Linda said. "We

can't let him think that Andy was the only one hanging around her room this morning."

"So let's go down and tell the Sheriff," Bob suggested. "I think he's just arriving." He pointed towards the parking area of the Inn.

The next two hours seemed endless. Andy was searched, as was his room and also the areas of the Inn where he'd been working. Mrs Barker's room was searched extensively, too, but there was no sign of the diamonds anywhere.

The Sheriff consented to look at the boot print, but by the time they climbed the narrow trail again, the wind had so badly blurred the print that he only shrugged. "I've heard about the Rogerses' troubles," he said, "but I don't see what some practical joker on a dude ranch could have to do with a theft here."

"It was the same print, Sheriff, I'm sure of it," Linda told him, unable to answer his question.

"That doesn't clear your friend Greer," the Sheriff answered as they returned to Andy and Mr O'Roarke.

"But it does show that someone else could be interested in the diamonds, doesn't it?" Bob asked.

The Sheriff sighed. "I'm not going to arrest your friend, anyway," he said. "There's not enough evidence at the moment. However, he's not going to be able to leave the resort till those diamonds turn up."

"But he didn't take them," Linda began.

"Then you'll just have to prove that someone else did," the Sheriff told her, his eyes cold.

Linda wanted to protest, but the Sheriff's gaze stopped her. "Well, if you don't have any questions for us, I guess we'd better be on our way," Larry said, looking sadly at Linda.

Bob nodded. "We were on our way to Scotty's Castle, so . . ."

Mr O'Roarke looked up, then consulted his watch. "Oh, dear," he said. "I'm afraid you won't have time for that this afternoon. It's a fifty-four-mile drive and the Castle closes at five. I'm terribly sorry we held you up so long."

"We can't go?" Kathy's voice expressed the disappointment they all felt.

Mr O'Roarke looked uncomfortable, and then he smiled. "Listen, I have an idea. The Inn offers a guided bus tour to Scotty's Castle several times weekly. The next one will be the day after tomorrow. Since we've made you miss your own tour, I'd be delighted to have you four as our guests."

"Well, I don't know," Linda began. "It depends on what Uncle Biff and Aunt Elaine have planned for us."

"Suppose we leave it for you to call us from Shadow Canyon as soon as you know your plans," Mr O'Roarke suggested. "I'll pencil your names in, but if you can't go, you can cancel. All right?"

"That's really very kind of you, Mr O'Roarke," Bob said. "We'll let you know this evening."

"The tour leaves at ten-thirty from in front of the Ranch registration desk. The Ranch is the area down there." He pointed towards the distant cluster of buildings. "You will return there about two-thirty."

"Sounds wonderful," Linda murmured. "Thank you very much for the offer."

Mr O'Roarke smiled at her for the first time since

he'd accompanied Mrs Barker to the pool area. "We owe you a debt, young lady," he told her. "Your questions kept Mrs Barker from making a terrible scene, and if young Greer is cleared, it will undoubtedly be your doing."

"Andy didn't take those diamonds, Mr O'Roarke," Bob said. "He just couldn't have."

"That will be up to the Sheriff to prove, but I certainly appreciate your defence of your friend. I don't like to think that any of our employees could do such a thing."

"We'd better be going," Larry said, taking Bob's arm. "Thanks again for the tour offer, Mr O'Roarke."

Bob's gaze was angry and Linda sensed that her brother was longing to snap at the man who'd just made it clear that his own concern for Andy Greer was only because Andy worked for him. They said nothing till they were all in the car and driving back down the hill from the resort.

"Poor Andy," Linda murmured.

"I wish we could take him to the ranch with us," Bob admitted.

"The Sheriff said he couldn't leave the resort," Kathy reminded them.

"Not even to come over on his day off," Larry agreed.

Bob sighed. "I guess we'll just have to see him the next time we're here," he said. "After our bus tour to Scotty's Castle."

"Then you think we should accept Mr O'Roarke's offer?" Linda asked.

"Why not?" Bob countered. "If they have a guide, we'll probably learn a great deal more than if we drive up there alone."

"What about now?" Larry asked. "Do you think we could go home by way of Devils Golf Course and Bad Water?"

"Good idea," Bob said. "I've read that the Golf Course is some of the roughest land in the country."

The detour proved fascinating as they climbed the delicately rugged formations of Devils Golf Course and gazed at the reflections in the shallow pool at Bad Water. Linda felt a pang of regret when the time came to return to the guest ranch and the problems that awaited them there.

"I wonder how Chica's feeling," she murmured, her mind moving ahead. "I really didn't like to leave her with a sore leg."

"She's probably all healed," Bob answered. "She wasn't limping much. I'm sure you'll be able to ride her tomorrow."

"Why would the ghost be here in Death Valley and at Shadow Canyon?" Larry asked.

"That's what we're going to have to find out," Bob said.

"How?" Kathy asked.

It was a question that held their attention for the remainder of the ride back to Shadow Canyon Guest Ranch but, even as Bob turned off the highway onto the now familiar road, they could find no answers. When they turned onto the road, however, something else caught their attention.

"Hey, do you suppose we're getting some new guests?" Bob asked, looking towards the nearby field.

"In a helicopter?" Linda was dubious.

"Important guests?" Larry suggested. "Did the

Rogerses say anything about expecting anyone?"

Linda shook her head. "Aunt Elaine said something about not having any reservations till Christmas."

"Well, whoever it was didn't stay long," Bob observed. "At least the helicopter is taking off."

"Hey, that's not just a helicopter," Linda gasped. "Look on the side. It's a rescue or a medical evacuation helicopter."

"Someone has been hurt!" Kathy moaned and the car leaped forward as Bob headed for the field as fast as he dared.

Linda said nothing, but she had an icy feeling that there was trouble ahead.

The Mysterious Landslide 6

The car bumped to a stop beside the ranch station wagon, and Linda was relieved to see both Biff and Elaine Rogers bracing themselves against the furious wind from the rising helicopter. It was a moment before she realized that although Sylvia and Jimmy were standing with their hosts, Mr Pendleton was nowhere to be seen.

"What happened?" Linda and her group chorused, jumping out of the car.

"It's Daddy," Sylvia wailed, throwing herself into Linda's arms and sobbing wildly.

"There was an accident on the ride," Aunt Elaine answered, her eyes full of misery.

"Oh, dear," Linda murmured. "What . . . ?"

"It was some sort of landslide," Uncle Biff answered. "Pendleton was caught in it. We don't think any bones were broken, but he has a terrible bump on his head. He was still unconscious when they took off."

"We have to go to him," Sylvia sobbed. "We have to be with Daddy."

"Honey, there wasn't room in the helicopter," Elaine Rogers said, patting the girl's shoulder. "I know you're worried, but we'll call the hospital in an hour and see what they have to say."

"Where are they taking him?" Bob asked.

"Las Vegas."

"I want to go, too," Jimmy cried, bursting into tears just as his sister had. "I want Daddy."

Bob and Linda exchanged glances. "Maybe we could . . ." he began.

"Oh, no." Aunt Elaine lifted a hand, stopping his words. "Sylvia, Jimmy, I'll tell you what. You go change from your riding clothes and pack overnight bags for yourself and for your father, too. Then I'll drive you into Las Vegas. We'll go to the hospital and then we'll find a motel for the night. How would that be?"

The two children looked at each other, then turned and raced across the field towards their adobe cabin. Uncle Biff turned to his wife. "Are you sure you want to do that, Elaine?" he asked.

"What else can we do?" she replied. "The accident happened on our property and those children lost their mother less than a year ago. They're too frantic to be content with phone calls. Besides, I'm sure their father is going to be worried about them as soon as he wakes up."

"But—"

"You can take care of things here, can't you?" Elaine Rogers asked. "There will just be the five of you."

"Six," her husband corrected. "Wayne is here, too."

Aunt Elaine shrugged. "Whatever. It will only be for a day or two. I'd better go throw a few things in a suitcase. I have a feeling that Sylvia will need some help getting things organized for herself and her father and brother."

Linda smiled. "I'll go and help her," she offered. "Packing is something that I've had a lot of experience doing."

"Is there anything we can do?" Bob asked.

"Well, you might try to find Wayne," Uncle Biff suggested. "He came riding in to tell me about the accident and I haven't seen him since. He didn't even go out with me in the car when I got Pendleton."

"Right away," Bob promised.

"Well, I'd better go help Sylvia," Linda said. "Check Chica for me, will you, Bob?"

Her brother nodded, getting back in the car. "Come on, Sis, I'll give you a ride."

Linda found Sylvia sitting in the middle of the cabin, which was totally cluttered with a mixture of clothing and other belongings. "I don't know what to take," she wailed. "Daddy always does all this."

"I'll help you," Linda offered, giving instructions.

As she worked, Jimmy emerged from the small second bedroom, his face still streaked with tears. "What are you doing here?" he asked.

"Helping you get ready to go," Linda answered. She then asked, "What happened on the ride, anyway?"

"It was my fault," Jimmy replied, his face darkening again as tears filled his grey eyes. "All my fault."

"Oh, I doubt that," Linda said. "Why don't you just tell me what happened."

There was a moment of silence, and then the boy took a deep breath and dropped onto the gingham-covered couch. "I saw the ghost," he said.

"You did?" It took all of Linda's self-control to keep from turning around to look at him. "Are you sure?"

"Well, I saw something," Jimmy amended. "It was after lunch. We were riding through the canyon and I saw something up on the rim. I tried to tell Dad and Mr Upton, but they just laughed, so . . ." His voice broke.

"So he climbed up anyway," Sylvia snapped, her voice angry. "He just left his horse and started up and, of course, Daddy had to go after him and that's when the landslide started."

"The ghost started it," Jimmy broke in.

"You started it," Sylvia accused. "You were up there."

Jimmy began to cry again, sounding far younger than ten. "I didn't," he sobbed. "I didn't, Sylvia, honest. I was just going after the ghost and he saw me and that's when he started the landslide."

"What did the ghost look like?" Linda asked, determined to distract the two as she packed the rest of their belongings in their suitcase.

"It was all dark and lumpy," Jimmy answered. "I thought it was a rock at first, but then it moved and I was sure it was a wolf or something hiding up in the rocks."

"Are you sure it wasn't?" Linda asked.

"Wolves don't have faces," Jimmy snapped, his tears dry now. "It had eyes, Linda, and a funny nose, kind of hooked like a parrot's beak."

"You were that close?" Linda gasped.

"It was looking down at me just before the slide started."

Linda started to ask another question, but a horn sounded outside the cabin and Sylvia ran to the window. "We have to go," the young girl said, "that is Mrs Rogers."

"Tell your father to get well soon," Linda called after them.

After they drove away, Linda went to check on Chica, but she hesitated at the door of the barn, remembering only too well what had happened to her the night before. Had her "ghost" been the same one Jimmy claimed to have seen? It seemed quite likely. But if Jimmy was right about the ghost, that meant that this time it had gone far enough to actually injure someone—and that was frightening.

"Come on in," Bob called from the shadowy interior. "Chica is fine. I was just feeding both of our horses."

"Her leg is better?" Linda went into Chica's stall to examine the filly's fetlock.

Bob leaned on the stall door. "She and Rocket were racing around the corral when I got here and she didn't have a trace of a limp."

"Then there's no reason why we can't ride out to Shadow Canyon tomorrow, is there?" Linda asked.

"Shadow Canyon?"

"That's where the landslide happened."

"You think there was something suspicious about the landslide?" Bob asked, frowning. "Mr Upton just said that they were in the canyon and Jimmy climbed up a cliff and started the slide. Isn't that what happened?"

"Not according to Jimmy," Linda answered, getting to her feet and brushing the straw from her knees. "He says that the ghost started the slide."

"*Our* ghost?" Bob sounded dubious.

"That's why I want to go out and investigate," Linda replied, giving Chica a final pat.

"Well, I guess we'd better get up to the house and see what Larry and Kathy are doing," Bob said.

"I hope they're cooking dinner." Linda giggled. "I didn't think it was possible, but I'm hungry again."

"Me, too," Bob agreed, then frowned. "That's really awful about Mr Pendleton, you know. I feel sorry for Sylvia and Jimmy."

Linda nodded. "Where's Mr Upton?" she asked as they neared the main house. "Is he going to be here for dinner?"

Bob shook his head. "He told me about the slide, and then he took off in his car. He said he'd taken care of the horses, but I checked and the water trough in the corral was almost dry, so I refilled it."

"I suppose he could have been upset about the accident," Linda suggested.

"Maybe," Bob agreed, but without really believing it.

In spite of their concern about Mr Pendleton, the evening proved to be a pleasant one. Though no cook had been hired, there was a roast in the oven and Kathy had produced a frozen pie from the freezer and put it in to bake. While they all worked in the big kitchen, Bob told Uncle Biff about their day's adventures at the Furnace Creek Inn.

"Good heavens, your friend has been accused of stealing?" he asked, upset. "But that's terrible. You
must help him."

"We'd like to, Uncle Biff," Linda said, "but there doesn't seem to be much we can do."

"Well, there was a boot print," Uncle Biff reminded her.

"I'd swear it was the same as the one we found in the barn last night," Linda replied, "but I don't know what that means. What would your ghost be doing at Furnace Creek Inn stealing diamonds?"

"Maybe a better question would be why is a person who steals diamonds haunting a little spread like this?" Uncle Biff asked, his face lined and weary. "Why would anyone try to drive us out of business? We certainly aren't a threat to anyone."

"Jimmy claims that the ghost started the landslide today," Linda said and filled everyone in on the details of his story.

"That's wild," Uncle Biff commented when she finished. "I didn't see anything at the canyon that looked like a ghost when I went out to get Pendleton."

"We thought maybe we could go there in the morning and look around," Linda said.

"It's a nice ride," he agreed, "and you're welcome to use whichever horses you want, but do be careful. I've had just about all the accidents I can take. If anyone else gets hurt out here, I'm going to sell out—retirement or not."

"What time did the landslide happen?" Linda asked, her mind suddenly busy.

"I don't know, probably sometime around two-thirty or three. They rode the long trail to the canyon and had lunch by the spring before riding into the canyon itself. Wayne got back fast because he came straight across country."

"What's the problem, Sis?" Bob asked.

"I was just trying to figure out if there was enough time for our watcher on the ledge to get from Furnace Creek to Shadow Canyon," Linda answered, "and it doesn't sound like it."

"Oh, I don't know," Uncle Biff said. "If he knew where he was going, you could drive from one to the other in, say, an hour, maybe a little longer. Why?"

Linda shrugged. "The boot prints seem to connect what happened to me last night to what occurred at the Inn today, and if Jimmy really saw what he said he did . . ." She let it trail off.

"Then we should find some boot prints tomorrow," Larry finished for her.

They all nodded. Then, Uncle Biff changed the subject. "Hadn't you better call the Inn and let them know about the bus trip?" he asked.

Bob snapped his fingers. "I'd forgotten all about it," he admitted. He looked at the other three. "What do you think?" he asked. "Do we accept or should we stay here on the ranch?"

"I think you should accept," Uncle Biff said before anyone else could answer. "They offer a nice tour and there's certainly nothing to do here. I mean, you'll be riding tomorrow, so the next day should be a good one to spend in Death Valley. After all, you did tell me how anxious you are to explore the area."

"That was before all this happened," Linda reminded him.

"It will give you a chance to talk to your friend again," Uncle Biff said. "He'll be needing your support. Maybe you could give him the name of my lawyer. Let me write it down for you."

Linda swallowed hard, feeling the weight of his words. "He is going to need a lot of help," she admitted. "I don't think that Sheriff cares a bit about clearing Andy. We're going to have to do it ourselves—somehow."

"Finding a ghost and a diamond thief, that's a tall order," Uncle Biff agreed, "but I think you can handle it."

"We have to," Bob said. "For Andy . . . and for you."

Shadow Canyon 7

The tour arrangements were made and dinner was long over by the time Elaine Rogers called. They waited anxiously as Uncle Biff talked to her. He was smiling as he replaced the receiver.

"She says that Pendleton regained consciousness in the helicopter just before they reached Las Vegas."

"Great," Bob said. "Is he going to be all right? Did he have any other injuries?"

"He has a lot of scrapes and bruises and maybe a cracked rib, but the head injury was the most serious and they're calling it a concussion—there's no sign of a fracture."

"When will they be back?" Linda asked.

"Well, that's the bad news." Uncle Biff's smile faded slightly. "It seems that the doctor wants him to spend at least a day in the hospital for further tests, so that means they won't be able to leave before tomorrow evening at the earliest."

"But . . ." Linda began. "Couldn't Aunt Elaine and the children come back in the morning?"

"She'd have to go back and pick up Mr Pendleton when he's released," Uncle Biff answered, "so she feels it would be better to stay over. Also, she has some business errands to take care of in Las Vegas, so she thought she'd use this time. Of course she's sorry she's not here with you, but . . ."

"We understand that Sylvia and Jimmy need her there," Linda assured him. "We just miss her."

"Well, we'll all have to keep busy, that way it won't be as lonesome. Now, for your ride to the canyon, did you want Wayne to guide you?"

Bob's eyes met Linda's as he shook his head. "Could you draw us a map, Uncle Biff?" he asked. "That way Mr Upton would be free to help you."

"Sure, that's no problem. I'll do it now." Uncle Biff got a piece of paper and sighed as he sank down at the table. "I just wish I could go with you," he said. "It seems that since I've been in the dude ranch business, I never have time to do any riding."

"Why don't you come?" Kathy asked.

"Someone has to be here in case Elaine calls or someone contacts us for a reservation." Biff Rogers looked sad. "Not that today's accident—if anyone hears about it—is going to help that situation."

"At least no one was seriously hurt," Linda reminded him.

"Not this time," Uncle Biff observed gloomily.

His mood didn't lift before they said goodnight, and Linda went to the room she and Kathy shared feeling nearly as depressed. Instead of helping their friends, she and Bob seemed to just be witnesses to their troubles. And the bad luck now extended to Andy, too.

The morning dawned beautifully clear and everything looked more hopeful as Uncle Biff helped the group select horses for Larry and Kathy. Rocket and Chica were prancing with eagerness when they led them out of the barn and Linda laughed at the filly as she saddled her.

"I think a long ride is just what we both need," she whispered into one golden ear. "And I'll even give you a chance to play horse detective. Think you could trail the ghost like a bloodhound?"

Chica rubbed her head against Linda's arm, then whinnied her answer.

"Sometimes I think she really understands you," Bob told Linda.

"This would be a good time for her to prove it," Linda agreed, patting the filly before she mounted. "Where's Uncle Biff?"

"He said he had to go up to the house for something," Bob answered. "We're supposed to wait."

"You have the map, don't you?" Larry asked.

"With three routes marked," Bob answered. "Which way do you want to go?"

"Let's leave the long route till the Pendletons are back," Linda suggested. "I keep thinking that our ghost is probably already out there removing every trace of his footprints or any other clue that he might have left behind."

"Here you are," Uncle Biff called, emerging from the house with two sets of bulging saddlebags. "You almost forgot your lunch."

"Lunch?" They all gasped, then looked at each other and began to giggle.

"We were so busy we didn't even think of it," Linda admitted.

"We sure would have remembered it by noon," Bob said. "You probably saved our lives, Uncle Biff."

"Just have a good day," he told them. "Don't hurry back or give a thought to anything except having a nice ride. Promise?"

They rode through the rough country . . .

"And you make dozens of new reservations," Linda told him, as they rode out of the ranch.

The ride was fun. The ranch horses were good-tempered and Chica danced along, full of her usual energy. The country was rough, with a forbidding grandeur in its crags and canyons. They had no trouble following the map that Biff had drawn, and it was nearing noon when they finally sighted the formation that marked the entrance to Shadow Canyon.

Bob reined in Rocket. "So what do you want to do, Sis?" he asked. "Explore the bottom or the top first?"

"How about lunch?" Larry suggested.

Linda laughed. "Good thinking," she agreed. "Then maybe we should split up. Two of us go into the canyon and two of us on the canyon rim, that way we can check both ends of the slide at the same time."

"That makes sense," Bob agreed.

"Isn't there supposed to be a spring near the canyon entrance?" Kathy asked.

"According to the map there is," Bob replied, "and just in time, too. The horses must be thirsty after such a long ride."

The spring was easy to find, since it was the only spot in the area that had grass and bushes growing around it. They let the horses drink, then unsaddled them and let them run loose in the entrance of the canyon while they opened the saddlebags Uncle Biff had prepared for them.

"Do you think he was expecting us to have company?" Linda asked as she unpacked piles of sandwiches, packets of biscuits, a can of peaches, spoons and dishes, a plastic bag of fresh raw vegetables, apples and pears, and two flasks of milk.

"He's used to packing for bigger groups, I guess," Bob answered.

"We can always eat what's left for dinner," Kathy suggested hopefully.

"You just don't want to cook," Bob teased.

"We could always give you and Larry a turn," Linda countered with a grin.

"Only if you're willing to eat whatever we cook," Bob warned.

"That's not fair," Kathy protested, but they all laughed as they attacked the piles of food.

"You know," Larry said when they'd finished eating. "I think it's strange that they'd have a landslide in this area, don't you?"

Bob followed his friend's gaze, then nodded. "I see what you mean," he observed. "There doesn't seem to be much loose rock. The sides of this canyon look pretty solid from here."

"So are you ready to explore?" Linda asked.

"Why don't you and I take the canyon floor, Linda?" Larry said. "Let Bob and Kathy go up on top."

"That sounds like a good idea," Bob agreed. "Give us time to get up there, and then we can ride parallel with you. That way we can find the exact spot of the slide from above and below and have a better chance of finding any clues."

Linda nodded. "You two go ahead then," she said. "Larry and I can clean up while we wait for you to get into position."

"You're sure it was on the right side of the canyon?" Bob asked.

"Jimmy said he was looking up to the right when he saw the ghost," Linda confirmed.

Chica whinnied in protest when Bob rode Rocket away, but Linda soothed her with a few bites of carrot and apple. "They aren't going far, girl," she assured her. "We'll all ride back together. We just have to do a little investigating now."

"Time for you to become a detective, horse," Larry teased, petting the filly, too.

Chica nodded her head vigorously, her snowy mane flying.

"I think she likes the idea," Linda said, giggling. "After all, she has a score to settle with the ghost. He's the one who caused her to hurt her leg."

"So let's go and get him," Larry suggested. Looking up, Linda saw that Kathy and Bob were nearing the canyon rim.

The canyon was very narrow, with high sheer cliffs rising on both sides to cast the deep shadows that had given it its name. They rode into the canyon single file, Linda leading the way. Because of the steepness of the sides, they had only occasional glimpses of the riders above, and Linda felt a chill that had little to do with the shade cast by the walls.

She forced herself to concentrate on the canyon side to her right, studying it, trying hard to find a clue or to spot the formation Jimmy had seen that had looked to him like a ghost. They were well into the canyon before she saw the fresh scar of the landslide.

"We've spotted the slide area," Larry called from behind her. "See anything up there, Bob?"

They heard the soft sounds of hooves above, and in a moment Bob was visible on the lip of the canyon. "Nothing but hard rock," he answered. "And car tracks. But they could be from the station wagon when Uncle Biff came to get Mr Pendleton."

"See anything ghostly?" Kathy asked, joining Bob.

Linda touched her heels to Chica's sides to urge her forward, but the filly refused to move. "Something is scaring Chica," she called, urging the filly more strongly. Chica stamped her feet and danced sideways a little, but she refused to take a single step forward.

"Maybe if I ride ahead of you," Larry suggested. "Most horses will follow another horse, even if they won't go first."

Linda nodded, not pleased by Chica's refusal, yet trusting her horse enough not to judge her harshly for it. She tightened the reins, backing the golden palomino off the trail and deeper into the shadows. As she did so, her eye was suddenly caught by two things: a darkness high under the curl of the canyon wall; and, at the same time, the gleam of something silvery, like a cobweb that crossed the trail at about the height of a horse's chest.

"Larry, wait," she shouted, but it was too late. The horse was already moving and in a moment a cascade of rock and broken shale came roaring down the canyon wall, nearly catching the frightened horse and rider as Larry jerked his mount back out of the way in the nick of time.

"What the devil?" Bob leaned over the canyon rim. "What happened? Are you two all right?"

"I'm fine," Linda assured him. "Larry?" Her brown eyes were troubled as she watched the handsome young man soothe his startled horse, then dismount to check the animal for injuries.

"Seems to be fine," he answered. "He's got a couple of scrapes from the rocks that hit him, but nothing serious. You saved us both from getting hit." He looked up at her. "How did you know?"

Linda took a deep breath. "There was something across the trail. It looked like a cobweb in the sun, only . . . It must have been a fine wire." She slipped off Chica and moved to check the chest of the roan that Larry had been riding. "See, he hit it," she said, pointing to a very fine welt in the animal's well-groomed hide. "Not hard enough to cut him, but just enough to make a mark." She drew a finger over part of the line and it vanished, though the horse winced at her touch.

"Do you think it's safe to climb up there now?" Larry asked, looking nervously at the canyon wall.

Linda peered towards the dark bulk she'd seen in the flash before the slide, but now there was only a hollow with a slightly different coloured soil showing. "Let's ask Chica," she suggested, leading the filly forward.

Chica followed without hesitation.

"She must have seen the wire," Larry said. "Or sensed that something was wrong, anyway."

"Good girl," Linda told the filly, putting her arms around the sleek neck and hugging her as Chica blew softly through her nostrils and nuzzled the top of her head. "You saved us from what could have been serious injury."

There was a clattering of hooves behind them and Bob and Kathy rode in. After a moment of explaining, Linda led them up the rough canyon wall towards the hollow. It was difficult going with the new coating of loose gravel, rock, and dirt; but they made it eventually.

It took only a few seconds for Bob to locate a thin piece of plywood with some heavy wire still attached to it. The inside of the board was heavily coated with dirt and rocks, and he easily found the spot where the board had been set.

"What do you think?" Linda asked.

"That someone set a very neat little trap," Bob answered. "Or probably more than one."

"What do you mean?" Kathy asked.

"This slide is in a different spot than the one that hurt Mr Pendleton," Linda answered for him, as she looked back down towards the canyon floor.

Bob nodded. "Not exactly ghostly," he commented, "but it certainly is a dirty trick."

Larry sighed. "I don't really think the slide itself would have seriously injured me," he said, "but a frightened horse can do a lot of damage in a confined area like this canyon."

"Especially with inexperienced riders," Linda agreed. "Plus, the other slide may have released more rock."

"Well, I guess this proves for sure that someone is deliberately trying to ruin Uncle Biff and Aunt Elaine," Bob observed with a sigh. "Unfortunately, it doesn't tell us a thing about who is doing it."

"This does," Linda said as she examined an area of earth off to one side of the hollow.

"What does?" Larry and Bob asked together as Kathy scrambled up to peer over Linda's shoulder.

"The clover leaf!" Kathy gasped.

Linda nodded. "Our ghostly man from the barn and the ledge has been here, too," she confirmed. "Or at least someone with the same boot heel has been. It appears as though the rock slide took the rest of the print. Let's look around. Maybe we can also find some other clues."

After a fruitless search, Larry finally asked, "So what do we do now?"

Bob shrugged. "Go back to the ranch and tell Uncle Biff, I suppose," was all he could suggest. "Maybe he'll be able to think of something."

Linda could tell from his expression that he had little hope of that. "Maybe we should talk to Mr Upton," she suggested as they rode across the open plain towards the distant ranch buildings.

"If he's around," Bob answered without enthusiasm.

"You don't like him, do you?" Linda asked.

"I don't trust him," Bob replied, and then looked embarrassed. "I guess I'm just used to being around real horsemen like Bronco and Cactus Mac. Wayne Upton doesn't seem right for the wrangler of a guest ranch."

Linda looked at her brother. "That doesn't make him guilty of any of this," she reminded him. "Besides, his boot prints are all wrong."

"I know," Bob admitted. "I even checked the soles of his dress boots while we were in the bunkhouse talking about the accident."

"So he's not our ghost?" Kathy asked.

"Afraid not."

They rode on in silence, wondering how they were going to help their friends when every clue they'd found seemed to lead to the same dead end. It was enough to spoil the beauty of the day and the joy of riding across the open plain.

Scotty's Castle 8

By the time the riders had unsaddled and rubbed down the horses, fed all four, and put Rocket and Chica into their stalls, the day was dimming towards evening. Linda sighed and pushed back her dark hair. "Maybe you two should go check the bunkhouse and see if Mr Upton will be joining us for dinner," she said. "Kathy and I can go on to the house and see what Uncle Biff has been doing."

"I thought he'd be down to ask us what we found," Bob commented, a little frown marring his even features.

"Maybe he's waiting for a phone call," Kathy suggested.

"Or he might not have seen us ride in," Larry added.

"We'll know in a minute," Linda said, heading across the rough grass towards the bulk of the big old ranch house.

There were no lights behind the deep-set windows, but the rear door was unlocked and the two girls entered without question. Kathy stopped inside the kitchen and sniffed questioningly. "I don't smell dinner cooking," she groaned.

"Uncle Biff," Linda called. "We're home."

There was no answer and, after a moment, she crossed to the counter, suddenly spotting a white square. The note was short:

Kids,

Have been called away on business. Will be late, so go ahead with dinner and don't wait up for me. We'll talk after your tour tomorrow, if not before.

Love,
Uncle Biff.

"Well, that explains why there isn't any dinner cooking," Linda said, handing the note to Kathy. "Looks like we're on our own again."

Kathy sighed. "I don't suppose you'd settle for eating the leftovers of our lunch."

"Even you can't be that desperate to avoid cooking," Linda replied. "Let's look in the freezer and the pantry."

"Maybe I can find a couple of cans of chilli," Kathy suggested, heading for the pantry.

A few minutes later, Bob and Larry came in. Linda handed them the note, then returned her attention to the interior of the refrigerator. "What did Upton have to say?" she asked over her shoulder.

"Nothing," Bob answered. "He's still gone. At least his car isn't parked beside the bunkhouse anymore."

"Then I guess there will be just us for dinner," Kathy said from the pantry doorway. "Anyone for chilli burgers?"

Though they all tried, it was not a happy evening and Linda was relieved when they agreed to leave the dying fire and go to bed. They'd talked and talked about the two mysteries that confronted them, but nothing they'd said had offered any answers.

Morning came with more sunshine and Linda went yawning to the kitchen to start breakfast. Bob, Larry, and Kathy responded to the scents of bacon and eggs, but there was no sign of Uncle Biff even when they sat down at the table.

"Do you think I should go tap on Uncle Biff's door?" Bob asked, frowning at the empty chair.

"If he got in very late, he might be sleeping in," Linda suggested. "He did say in his note that he would see us after we got back from our tour."

"I suppose this is sort of a vacation for him," Kathy observed. "I mean since he doesn't have any guests to take care of."

"How about leaving early for Furnace Creek?" Linda suggested. "We could stop by the Inn and talk to Andy before we meet the bus."

"Hey, that's a good idea," Bob agreed. "We can give him the name of Uncle Biff's lawyer so he can call him."

"Maybe by now he's been cleared," Linda said.

"You think the Sheriff might have solved the theft?" Kathy asked, buttering fresh toast.

"We can hope," Larry said, but doubt was in his voice.

"If we just had more of a description of the man," Linda murmured. "A beaky nose isn't enough to go on."

"Mrs Barker wasn't any help either," Bob rumbled. "At least Andy said he was sure that the man wasn't a guest at the Inn."

"I wonder if he was ever a guest here," Linda mused. "If we had a better description we could ask Uncle Biff."

"I keep thinking about the landslide in the canyon

yesterday," Larry said. "That was really a trap."

"Well, we released it, so that's not a problem anymore," Kathy said as she helped herself to more eggs.

"No, that one isn't, but I wonder how many more there are," Larry continued. "I mean, how do we know there aren't little booby traps all over this ranch?"

Linda swallowed hard. "I guess we don't," she admitted.

"I think we'd better talk to Uncle Biff about that when we get back," Bob said, finishing his food. "However, at the moment, Larry and I should go and check the horses. We have to feed Rocket and Chica, and I don't trust that Upton to take care of the ranch stock."

"We'll clean up here and meet you at the barn," Linda agreed. "I want to make sure yesterday's ride didn't reinjure Chica's leg."

There was still no sign of life from the direction of Uncle Biff's room when they'd finished cleaning, so Linda and Kathy let themselves out into the fresh air without having seen their host. Chica was already in the small corral with Rocket, and as they approached, the two horses were chasing each other around the dusty area, bucking and kicking with high spirits.

"I don't think you have to worry about Chica," Kathy observed with a grin. "She looks fine."

"I just want to be sure that she's in shape for the show in Las Vegas," Linda replied. "Since I'll be Aunt Elaine and Uncle Biff's representative, they're counting on me to make an impression so that people will remember the name Shadow Canyon Guest Ranch."

"You'll be terrific, don't worry," Kathy assured her.

Linda sighed. "Truthfully, I'm more worried about whether there will be a guest ranch to represent," she admitted, no longer smiling even though Chica had come over to be petted. "Larry was right, you know. What happened in Shadow Canyon could just be the beginning if we don't find out who is behind this."

"Hey, no grim faces," Bob said, coming out of the barn. "We're going on a tour of Scotty's Castle in Death Valley today and we're going to enjoy it."

"Everything all right there?" Linda asked, gesturing towards the barn.

"Mr Upton just came out to take care of the ranch horses," Larry answered. "And he promised that he would keep an eye on Rocket and Chica till we get back."

"Somehow that just doesn't fill me with confidence," Linda replied. But she did manage a smile, and as the four of them walked to the car, she felt a returning of her hope. Maybe, just maybe, the Sheriff might have found out something about the diamonds . . . and once he caught the thief . . . She was sure the two mysteries were somehow connected and she could only hope that one clue would lead them to a solution of both.

They arrived at the Inn in plenty of time for a visit with Andy. However, when they entered the lobby, Mr O'Roarke was not behind the desk and Andy wasn't anywhere to be seen in the dining room. Linda took a deep breath and approached the woman at the front desk.

"May I help you?" the woman asked with a smile.

"I was wondering if I might speak to Andy Greer," Linda began. "I thought he'd be in the dining room, but . . ." She stopped as the woman's smile faded.

"Are you friends of his?"

"My brother and I are," Linda answered. "We were here to visit him the day before yesterday and at that time Mr O'Roarke said . . ."

"You've spoken with Mr O'Roarke?"

Linda nodded. "Is he here?" she asked.

"Mr O'Roarke is at the Sheriff's office with Andy Greer," the woman answered, her tone changing. "They left several hours ago."

"They haven't arrested Andy, have they?" Bob asked, taking his place beside her.

The woman looked in both directions, then leaned forward, keeping her voice low. "Mrs Barker was threatening to sue the resort because Andy was still allowed to work, so Mr O'Roarke had no choice but to take him off duty. However, I don't know why the Sheriff wanted to talk to them again."

"The Sheriff?" Linda asked.

The woman nodded. "He called Mr O'Roarke this morning. They left right away."

"Will Andy be coming back here?" Bob inquired.

"As far as I know," the woman answered. "You can check later today."

Bob nodded. "We're going to the Scotty's Castle tour, so we'll come back here afterwards. Would you tell Andy that Linda and Bob Craig were here?"

"I'll tell him," the woman promised.

"So what do we do now?" Kathy asked as they went outside. "We've got an hour before we have to catch the bus."

"Why don't we explore the ranch area?" Bob suggested. "I think they have a museum or something. I picked up a brochure the day we came in for lunch and it sounds like they have all kinds of stuff."

"We might as well," Linda agreed. "There doesn't seem to be anything we can do here."

They spent the time at the Ranch happily. The Borax Museum with its display on the history of the area was interesting, and the boys were fascinated by Old Dinah, the steam tractor with its attached ore cars and the display of the original ore wagons that had been pulled through Death Valley by the twenty-mule teams.

Kathy and Linda did a thorough investigation of the general store. It held a fascinating collection of practical items, grocery and camping supplies, as well as souvenirs and gifts from all over the area.

Once aboard the bus, they were all entranced by the woman guide who regaled them with stories of the old prospectors, the fascinating characters who had explored and settled the area. It was from her that they learned of Albert Johnson, the man who built the Castle and shared it with his friend Walter Scott.

"No two men could have been more different than Johnson and Scott," the guide explained. "Mr Johnson was a rich, well-educated gentleman, while Mr Scott was something of a genial conman, living more by his wits than by his hard work. Still, when Mr Johnson invested in Scotty's mysterious Death

Valley gold mine, a friendship was born that lasted for a lifetime and, very likely, gave Mr Johnson many additional years of life, for the Valley's climate well suited his weak constitution.

"The Castle itself was mainly built to please Mr Johnson's wife, who hated most of the creatures of the desert and demanded a style of living at least close to what she'd left behind. Though it was Johnson's money and taste that went into the Castle, it was never known as anything but Scotty's Castle and is a wonderful memorial to Death Valley's most colourful character."

The woman continued with many stories of Scotty's life, but nothing she said prepared them for the size and grandeur of the frame and stucco buildings of the Castle complex. The tour, which was conducted by an attractive young girl, left them entranced with the wonder of the ornate and electronically elegant music room and fascinated by the charming imported tile that covered much of the kitchen area.

"I could spend a week exploring that place," Linda commented as they walked out through the heavy wooden gates that guarded the Castle's courtyard.

"Maybe we can come again," Bob suggested. "If we're going to the Inn to talk to Andy, there's no reason why we can't come back here."

"Andy," Linda murmured, her happy mood fading. She sighed. "I just wish I knew how we could help him."

"Maybe he'll have more to tell us this afternoon," Bob suggested.

That thought stayed in both their minds through the remainder of the tour and spoiled some of their enjoyment of the afternoon. Linda was rather relieved when the bus finally stopped at the Furnace Creek Ranch again and they could get in their own car and drive back up to the Inn. She was pleased to find Mr O'Roarke standing behind the desk.

Bob hurried forward to ask, "Is Andy all right, Mr O'Roarke? We stopped by this morning and the desk clerk said you'd taken him to the Sheriff's office."

"I'm afraid things didn't go well," Mr O'Roarke said, his welcoming smile fading.

"What do you mean?" Bob asked.

"Your friend has been arrested." Mr O'Roarke looked miserable. "I did everything I could to keep it from happening, but there simply wasn't a shred of evidence that anyone else is involved and there has been a new development."

"What's happened?" Linda asked.

"It seems that Andy made a big deposit in his savings account the night after the diamonds were taken. He must have sold some of them." O'Roarke spoke quickly.

"But that's crazy," Bob said. "Andy didn't steal the stupid diamonds, so how could he have sold them? Besides, he was here on the resort, wasn't he?"

"He could have slipped away for a couple of hours," Mr O'Roarke replied. "Or maybe he had an accomplice we don't know about."

"I don't believe it," Linda said.

"The Sheriff got a phone tip," Mr O'Roarke continued. "He checked Andy's account. The deposit was made all right. Where else would Andy get five thousand dollars?" He paused, then added, "They're searching the resort and Andy's room again now, looking for the rest of the jewels."

Bob started to turn away, then asked, "Are you saying that you believe Andy took those diamonds?"

Mr O'Roarke shrugged. "I can't argue with the evidence."

"There has to be another explanation," Linda protested, "and when we find it, you're going to be very ashamed of yourself for ever believing something like that about Andy." She turned on her heel and left the lobby, the other three following her.

It wasn't till they were all in the car and on their way home that Bob spoke. "That was a great speech you gave O'Roarke, Sis," he said, "but how are we going to clear Andy?"

Linda sighed, then shook her head. "I wish I knew," she answered. "I guess all we can do is ask Uncle Biff to call his lawyer for Andy."

"I hope it's enough," Bob observed, but his voice held no more hope than hers had, and the trip back to the ranch was a rather quiet one as they all tried to think of ways they could help Andy.

Vanished! 9

When they drove into the ranch yard, Linda was so depressed about Andy that she just got out of the car with the others and made her way into the house. It wasn't till she reached the kitchen that she realized how still the building was—how empty.

"Uncle Biff," Bob shouted. "Uncle Biff, where are you?"

Silence was the only reply.

"Where can he be now?" Linda asked, looking around the kitchen, half expecting to see another note propped up against the breadbox or the biscuit jar; but the only things still on the counter top were the few dishes that they'd left out.

"It doesn't look like he's even been here," Kathy commented.

"You're right," Bob admitted. "I'm going to check his room to see if he's there."

Linda moved slowly around the kitchen, then looked in the refrigerator, noting that none of the food appeared to have been touched. Bob returned, his face grave. "I don't think he's been here," he said. "The bed is all made and the place is neat, the way Aunt Elaine leaves things, not the way Uncle Biff would."

"But where in the world . . ." Linda began, then stopped as the phone rang. She hurried to answer it, sure that it would be Uncle Biff calling to tell them where he was.

"Biff?" It was Elaine Rogers.

"This is Linda, Aunt Elaine," Linda answered.

"Oh, hello, dear, how are you?" Her voice sounded distracted.

"We're fine. How are you and how is Mr Pendleton getting along?"

"That's why I'm calling. Mr Pendleton is doing fine, but it will be at least tomorrow before the doctors will release him and I have a morning appointment at the bank, so I'll be here another night. Is Biff there?"

"No, I don't think so," Linda replied. "In fact, Aunt Elaine, we don't know where he is. There was a note waiting for us when we got back from our ride last night and . . . well, he didn't get up with us this morning, so . . ." She let it trail off, hating to upset Aunt Elaine, yet too worried about Uncle Biff not to say anything.

"What do you mean he didn't get up with you this morning?" Aunt Elaine demanded.

"We thought maybe he came home very late, but . . . " Linda swallowed hard. "Bob just checked the bedroom and he doesn't think the bed has been slept in."

"If it was made, it wasn't." Aunt Elaine's voice sounded strained.

"Do you have any idea where he could have gone, Aunt Elaine?" Linda asked, frightened by the turn of the conversation.

"He didn't say anything in his note?"

"Just that he was called away on business and might be late getting back, but he said he'd talk to us after our tour, so—"

"Have Bob run out to the garage and see if the car is gone," Aunt Elaine suggested.

Linda did as she was told, then gave Aunt Elaine a brief report on all that had happened. She finished just as Bob returned. Linda handed him the phone without question.

"Aunt Elaine, the car's still there," Bob told her. He listened for a moment, then said, "We'll go out and check the ranch as soon as I hang up and I'll call you back the minute we come in, okay? Try not to worry."

"Do you really think Uncle Biff went out riding yesterday afternoon?" Linda asked as Bob turned from the phone.

"How else would he have left, if he didn't take the car?" Bob questioned.

"Maybe Upton would know," Larry suggested.

"He didn't say anything this morning," Bob reminded him.

"This morning we didn't ask him if he knew where Mr Rogers had gone," Larry answered.

"Okay, Larry, you go and ask him," Bob said. "I'm going to call the lawyer and see what he can do to help Andy."

"Kathy and I will start saddling the horses," Linda volunteered, glad that they'd chosen to wear their western clothing on the tour and didn't have to take time to change.

"I won't be long," Bob assured her. "There aren't too many hours of daylight left."

Linda was halfway across the open area before she realized that neither Rocket nor Chica was in the corral. "I wonder why Mr Upton put the horses inside," she murmured, more to herself than to Kathy, who was trotting beside her.

The barn was quiet when they entered, but

Rocket's bay head appeared over his stall door immediately and he whickered a greeting. Kathy went to pet him while Linda continued on to Chica's stall.

"Hey, Chica," she called. "Wake up, we're back and . . ." Her words died in her throat as she realized that the stall was empty. "Chica!" she called, looking around wildly, trying to believe that the wrangler had simply put the filly in another stall. But there was no bright palomino head appearing over any of the other stall doors and no whicker answered her.

"What's wrong?" Kathy asked, leaving Rocket to go to her friend.

"She's gone," Linda gasped. "Kathy, Chica is gone!"

"What's going on?" Bob asked, coming into the barn.

"Chica's not here," Linda answered, trying hard to control her panic.

"Did you find Mr Upton?" Kathy asked Larry as he joined them.

"He was in the bunkhouse," Larry replied as Bob went to put his arm around his sister. "He said that Mr Rogers left yesterday with some friends—in their car."

"Is something wrong?" Wayne Upton came into the barn.

"Where is my horse?" Linda demanded. "What have you done with Chica?"

"Isn't she in her stall?" Upton crossed to look. "That's where I put her a couple of hours ago."

"Well, she's not there now," Bob snapped. "Was anybody here?"

Upton shrugged. "I took a little nap, so I guess someone could have come, but I think I would have heard a car or something like that."

"Then where is she?" Linda demanded.

"Take it easy, Sis," Bob counselled. "Let's go out and see if we can spot any hoofprints. Chica has smaller hooves than most horses because she's part Arabian, so if she got loose and wandered off, we should be able to pick out her tracks."

"Sure, that's probably what happened," Upton agreed. "Horses are always getting loose and wandering off. I tell you—"

Linda stopped his words with a glare. "She opened her stall door and walked away," she mocked. "After neatly closing it behind her, of course."

"Come on, Sis." Bob half-dragged her outside and, once she was there, Linda joined in the circling search for hoofprints. It was several minutes before she found some in the softer soil near the garage.

"Over here," she called.

"Those are Chica's prints, all right," Bob agreed, after studying them. "Did you ride this way yesterday?"

Linda thought for a moment, then shook her head. "Not over here."

"Well, then, let's saddle up the horses and see where these lead," Larry suggested.

"She wasn't just wandering," Linda protested, moving along the trail of hoofprints that appeared and disappeared with the soil conditions. "She would have gone over to nibble on that big clump of grass if she'd been loose."

"Oh, you can't be sure of that," Upton told her, following them after having emerged from the barn. "Horses do strange things. You can't predict any—"

"Bob!" Linda's heart leaped, then dropped as she stood over the small damp spot where water had leaked from a faucet on the side of the garage.

"What is it?" Bob dropped to his knees.

"The ghost was here," Linda whispered as Larry and Kathy came to stare at the telltale boot print.

"What are you all looking at?" Upton asked, his expression changing to one of suspicion.

"You want to help me pick out a horse for Linda?" Bob asked before anyone else could speak. As he got up, his foot slid into the damp spot and destroyed the print. "If we're going after Chica, we'd better go right away."

"You want me to go with you?" Upton asked, his eyes going from one to the other doubtfully.

"No, I think it would be better if you go up to the house and call Aunt Elaine," Bob said. "Tell her about the men that picked up Uncle Biff. Otherwise, she's going to be frantic and she'll probably call the police. The motel number is on the pad."

Upton looked as though he'd like to argue, then shrugged. "Just give the girl the buckskin," he said, heading for the house without a backward glance.

Linda glared after him for a moment, then ran to help the others saddle the horses, frantic to go after Chica. In her heart she was very much afraid that she wasn't going to find her golden filly too easily.

The trail proved impossible to follow once they left the vicinity of the ranch buildings. The ground was hard and rocky or covered with sand that seemed to swallow all tracks as the wind washed over it. Soon they fanned out, staying within eyesight of each other, but combing the dozens of ravines that snaked through the rough ground as it rose towards the canyons and foothills.

The sun was nearly down when Bob whistled loudly, their agreed-upon signal. Linda rode towards him hopefully, but she could see that he was alone.

"We've got to give up for tonight, Sis," he told her. "It's going to be pitch dark out here in half an hour."

"But Chica . . ." Linda protested, as Kathy and Larry rode up to join them.

"We'll start looking at dawn tomorrow," Larry assured her. "But we could ride right by her tonight and not see her."

Linda wanted to argue, but she knew that they were right. Feeling weary and frightened, she allowed her mount to turn back towards the ranch. Chica was out somewhere, lost and probably frightened, and she longed to keep looking till she found her.

Only when they were riding in together did Linda remember to ask Bob what the lawyer had said.

"He promised he'd go right to the jail to see Andy and would call us this evening and let us know how he is," Bob answered.

"Did he sound hopeful?" Linda asked.

"Not really," was Bob's discouraging reply.

Dinner was a dismal meal and their mood wasn't lifted by the two phone calls they received. Aunt Elaine was worried and Upton's words hadn't reassured her. She couldn't think of anyone Biff might be with.

The lawyer's call was worse, and Bob's expression was grim as he turned from the phone. "They found a diamond hidden in a spot they hadn't searched the first time they were in Andy's room," he groaned. "Now they're sure he's guilty."

"But . . ." Linda began, then gave up, too heartsick to go on. It was a relief to just quietly go to bed and try to forget her fears in sleep.

Linda dreamed about Chica. She was riding her, but then all at once the filly was gone and she was walking through a thick forest, calling for her. Chica whinnied and . . . Linda sat up, suddenly wide awake. Had she heard a whinny?

Every nerve in her body quivered as her sharp ears caught the sound again. It was so distant that she couldn't actually be sure that the whinny was Chica's, but still . . . Linda slipped out of her bed, shoving her feet into trainers and picking up her warm dressing gown as she padded to the window.

The moon had risen and the area beyond was surprisingly light. Linda looked around, trying hard to see if her beloved palomino might be out there, but she couldn't see her. The whinny came again, a little louder this time, but very plaintive.

"Chica!" Linda whispered. She hurried out of the house, not bothering to wake any of the others, her heart pounding with excitement. The filly must have escaped from whoever had taken her, she decided. She was probably thirsty and hungry and very anxious for the security of her own stall and Rocket's friendly presence.

The night air was cold and Linda clutched her dressing gown more tightly around her, glad that she'd chosen to bring warm flannel pyjamas. Pausing to look around, she quickly spotted something moving in the distance and started running towards it, calling Chica's name.

Linda's breath was coming in gasps and her side ached with the pain of breathing before she slowed her running. It was only then that she realized that Chica wasn't trotting towards her. Horrified, she saw that the filly was limping awkwardly. Pain forgotten, Linda ran forward again and stopped the labouring animal by throwing her arms around the filly's neck.

"Oh, Chica, you poor darling," she sobbed against the warm, silky hide. "What did they do to you? My poor baby."

The filly nuzzled Linda's head and blew her warm breath in her mistress's dark hair. Linda held on to her for another moment, then forced herself to straighten up and look at Chica, even though she was terribly afraid of what she was going to see.

Chica continued to nuzzle Linda's shoulder as she bent to examine the filly's slender front legs. Then, suddenly, Linda began to laugh, almost hysterical in her relief. "Oh, Chica, they hobbled you," she gasped between giggles, her fingers shaking so that she had a difficult time unbuckling the hobbles and freeing the graceful filly.

Chica moved away from her, dancing a little as though she was relieved to be free of the trapping leather. Linda straightened up and looked around, wondering what she could use to lead the filly back to the safety of the barn, since Chica wore neither halter nor bridle.

She started to untie her dressing gown belt, thinking that she would tie it around the filly's neck and use that. But before she could do it, Chica swung around, her head up, ears pricked forward so sharply

Linda galloped after the hooded rider . . .

that their tips almost touched. Linda followed her gaze and saw that a horseman was approaching.

The person who'd stolen Chica? It seemed likely. Terrified of losing Chica again, Linda twisted her fingers in the filly's mane and vaulted desperately onto her sleek back. Chica bounced with excitement, then whinnied to the other horse. The other horse answered and the rider slowed.

Linda considered flight, but her curiosity was stronger than her fear. She stroked the filly's neck and talked to her, keeping her still as the horseman drew nearer.

"What do you want?" Linda demanded, peering at the rider.

He made no sound and Linda felt a chill wash over her as she realized that he was wrapped in some kind of dark, hooded robe—a robe that glowed faintly in the moonlight. "Who . . . who are you?" she gasped.

The creature laughed, an evil sound that filled the night and sent shivers along her spine. Then he reined his horse around and cantered away.

"You'll never know, will you?" he taunted over his shoulder.

Suddenly her fear turned to anger and she thought of Andy arrested and unable to prove his innocence, of Uncle Biff's losing this ranch, and of poor Mr Pendleton in the hospital. She pressed her hands against Chica's neck and leaned forward, digging her heels into the surprised filly's sides.

"Oh, yes, I will find out!" she shouted as she started after the rider.

Kidnapped! 10

At first the ghostly rider seemed too surprised to escape; then he appeared to realize that she was serious in her pursuit and he urged his horse into a gallop. He headed north into an area of the ranch that they'd not explored and Linda felt a chill of fear.

Chica ran easily after the other horse, but they didn't seem to gain on the beast. The filly's struggle to come back to the ranch in spite of her hobbles had obviously taken its toll of her strength, and Linda didn't urge her to increase her pace after the first few minutes.

"I should have called Bob and Larry," she told the filly. "But I wasn't sure that I'd really heard you. Besides I was so happy at getting my Chica back."

Chica snorted a sort of answer, then changed direction slightly as the rider ahead of them disappeared into the darkness of a canyon. Linda leaned back, slowing the well-trained filly, then shifted her weight to the right, directing Chica into the shadowy area.

The canyon floor was almost invisible to her eyes, but Chica seemed confident as she moved ahead, so Linda didn't stop her. Could this be where the diamonds were hidden? she asked herself, sure that the mysterious rider must also be the ghost who'd haunted the ranch and the watcher who'd robbed Mrs Barker.

Chica slowed, her dainty ears flipping forward and back, as though she was seeking some sound from Linda as well as still listening for the horse and rider ahead. Then she stopped, her warm body quivering slightly between Linda's knees.

"What's the matter, girl?" Linda whispered, suddenly conscious of the vast silence that surrounded them. There were no sounds of hoofbeats ahead.

Chica snorted again, then moved forward cautiously, her shod hooves sounding terribly loud in the night stillness of the canyon. Ahead, a horse whickered and Linda felt a little better. This must be the ghost's hiding place, she decided, stopping the filly with a single "Whoa".

Linda slid off the filly's sleek back and stood with her arm lightly around the horse's neck. What should she do? she asked herself, wishing again for the comforting assistance of Bob, Larry, and Kathy.

Should she turn back now and ride for help? It was a tempting idea, but she had a strong suspicion that the rider would vanish if she did. But how could she do anything alone? The rider had been a man and she still remembered the way he'd knocked her down in the barn, which told her he was both strong and determined. He wouldn't be easy to capture.

The restless horse ahead of them moved about, stamping its feet, then splashing in water, the sounds carrying loudly in the darkness. "That's it," Linda whispered to Chica. "We'll take his horse back to the ranch with us. He won't be able to go far on foot, and once Bob and Larry are after him . . . We'll be able to clear Andy and help Uncle Biff and Aunt Elaine."

Chica nuzzled her arm in apparent approval, then followed as Linda began tiptoeing along the rocky canyon floor. She could see very little in the area and was grateful that her dressing gown was dark, so that she, too, would be difficult to see; for she knew the rider must be somewhere close by watching for her.

"Stand, Chica," she whispered, knowing that the white-maned filly would be all too easy to spot. "I'll be right back."

Chica shifted her feet restlessly, but stayed where she was as Linda continued along the edge of the canyon alone. The other horse moved again and she realized that he was tied outside what looked like a rude shed.

Linda paused and peered at the scene for several minutes, watching the horse's nervous movements, the stillness of the rest of the area. She could see the bucket of water near the horse and the small pile of hay from which he occasionally took a bite. There was no sign of his rider.

Could the man have believed that he'd lost her when he turned into the canyon? she wondered. It seemed almost too much to hope for—but there was simply no one around. Linda cautiously moved closer to the horse, then hesitated, wondering if she dared try to look into the shed.

Deciding that she couldn't risk it, Linda was just reaching for the horse's reins when a cloud of black dropped over her head and upper body and hard arms came around her waist. She screamed in terror!

Almost at once there was a neigh of fury and she heard Chica's hooves pounding towards her. The arms released her and she was pushed to one side as Chica thundered by. Hope flowed through her and she battled the fold of cloth, trying to free herself. The blanket dropped away and she looked up just in time to see the faint gleam of starlight on a shiny gun barrel!

"Chica!" she screamed, realizing that the gun was pointing at the brave filly. Her hands scrabbled in the nearby earth and she found a small rock and threw it as hard as she could. It struck the man just as the gun went off.

"Chica, go to Bob!" Linda shouted. "Go to Bob!"

For a moment the startled horse hesitated, plainly torn between her desire to protect Linda and her obedience to her mistress's command, learned after the months of training that Linda had done since she'd brought the filly home. "Go, Chica!" she repeated as the man lifted his arm to shoot again. Linda launched herself at him.

The gun exploded once more, and a moment later Linda was slammed to the earth. Her head hit a rock and the darkness suddenly became complete and silent.

Linda awoke to pain. She tried to lift her hand to her aching head, but it didn't move. Frightened, she opened her eyes.

"Are you all right, Linda?" a wonderfully familiar voice asked.

"Uncle Biff?" Linda gasped, trying to move so she could see him.

"Right here, honey," he answered. "Are you hurt?"

Linda rolled over clumsily, realizing that her hands were tied. She wiggled and strained her way to a sitting position, ignoring the pounding in her head. "I'm fine," she managed. "Just a headache."

"What happened?" Uncle Biff asked. "How did you get here?"

Linda took a deep breath, feeling better with each passing moment. She told him as quickly as possible what had happened, starting with her capture, then going back through the past two days.

"Now, what about you?" she asked when she finished. "What are you doing here? Mr Upton said you'd gone off to visit some friends. And we found your note . . ."

"Some friends!" Uncle Biff growled. "And I didn't leave any note, believe me. I expected to be back long before you were."

"Someone forged it," Linda said, angry. "What happened to you?"

"I did something stupid," Uncle Biff admitted. "I got this phone call after you all rode off. A man said that he'd seen the ghost and if I'd meet him in town, he'd tell me everything he knew, even show me where the man was hiding."

"Did you believe him?" Linda asked.

Uncle Biff shook his head. "I had a hunch that it was some kind of trick, but I figured I'd be safe enough meeting him in town. Besides, I wanted to see who'd called. After all, I thought it was a clue to our mysterious ghost."

He stopped again, but this time Linda didn't question him, she was too busy worrying about Chica. Had the filly escaped? Where had the bullet gone that last time she'd heard the gun fire? She shuddered at the thought that Chica might have been hit and hurt—or worse.

"They were waiting for me about three miles down the highway," Uncle Biff began again. "They waved me down and once I'd stopped, they pulled a gun and ordered me into their car."

"They?"

"There were two men. One short and rather dumpy looking, the other about my height with dark hair and a nose like a parrot's beak. The short one tied me and then he left in my car. The other man drove me out here and I've been here ever since."

"A beaky nose . . . like the man Andy saw?"

Uncle Biff nodded. "But it could be a coincidence, Linda."

She sighed, then looked around. "Where are we?" she asked.

"Red Rock Canyon," Uncle Biff answered. "This is a mine entrance or, rather, this is a cave. The mine starts around that bend. It's only about thirty feet deep. Someone—maybe our ghost—has enclosed the cave entrance with a lean-to front and door."

Linda squirmed around. "Do you think you could untie my hands?" she asked.

"I don't know," he answered. "I'll sure try, but my fingers are pretty stiff and swollen from being tied up here so long."

"Well, maybe I can untie you," Linda suggested. "Let's get our backs to each other."

It took many agonizing minutes and her wrists were chafed and aching by the time she managed to loosen the ropes on Uncle Biff's wrists so he could pull himself free. Once he'd rubbed the feeling back into his hands, he quickly untied her.

"Now let's see if we can get out of here," he whispered, moving across the cave to the only wooden wall, the one that held the door. He tried it cautiously, then with more energy. But it refused to budge.

"Locked?" Linda asked.

"More likely braced, or maybe barred," Uncle Biff replied. "At least there wasn't a lock on it when he brought me in."

"Do you think he's out there?" Linda asked.

Uncle Biff shrugged and moved across to where the candle burned low. "It's hard to tell," he admitted. "He usually just comes once a day and leaves food. Tonight is the first time he's made a second trip."

"So what do we do now?" Linda asked.

Uncle Biff shook his head. "Maybe we can wait till he comes with our food. If I could hit him or something . . ."

"How long have I been here?" Linda asked.

"An hour, maybe two. My watch ran down yesterday."

"Did you hear anything, I mean just before he brought me in?"

"Two shots. Hoofbeats."

Linda expressed a sigh of relief—maybe Chica escaped.

"And afterwards?" she asked.

"Nothing for a little while, then . . . hoofbeats." Biff grinned at her. "You think that means he left?"

Linda looked around. "I know how we can find out," she said, pointing to the wall.

Biff followed her gaze and then nodded. "That's a heavy door," he observed, "but that wall doesn't look as strong. I'll bet they just used scrap wood."

Linda followed him, holding the candle as Biff examined the boards, testing the strength of each one before he finally selected a spot. "Stand back, Linda," he ordered. He then lifted his foot and began kicking the wall.

The first blow set the entire wall shuddering, and dust flew from every chink in the wood. The second kick brought the screech of tearing wood, and each subsequent blow spread the cracks wider, splitting the old board and letting in a current of cold, fresh air.

"You're doing it," Linda shouted as Uncle Biff sank down on the floor to rest.

"If I'd known I was going to be kicking down walls, I would have worn boots," he muttered, rubbing his leg and ankle. "That wood is hard."

"Maybe I can help," Linda offered, kicking at the board herself. But she lacked the strength and each blow deepened her headache. She dropped to the floor beside Uncle Biff.

They sat quiet for several minutes, and then he got up and attacked the wall again, finally splintering the board and opening a definite hole. He examined the boards above and below it. "I don't think I'm going to be able to break any more of them," he groaned.

Linda went over and pulled the splintered wood away, peering out at the night. Her field of vision was restricted, but she could see that the horse was no longer tied out in front. Nothing moved in the starlit canyon. She could hear no sounds beyond the breeze whining around the rocks and stirring the grass and brush.

"I think I can get through this," she told Uncle Biff, wiggling her shoulders through the opening. The rough edges of the wood caught in her dressing gown, but the dressing gown's thickness protected her as she did her best to squirm her hips through the space.

"Let me help you," Uncle Biff said, catching her feet, wrapping the dressing gown around them and supporting her weight as she slid out.

Linda landed in a heap on the rocky ground. She lay still for a moment, listening, half-expecting to see her captor looming out of the night—but there was nothing.

"Are you all right?" Uncle Biff's voice made her jump.

"I'm fine," Linda answered. "Let me see if I can open the door for you." She scrambled to her feet. It took her only a moment to lift the heavy wooden bar from the brackets that secured the door. It swung open and Uncle Biff emerged, walking stiffly, but with a grin that reflected even in the dim light from the stars.

He took several deep breaths, then laughed. "I can't believe this," he said. "We're actually outside!"

"So now what?" Linda asked, looking around and feeling a further easing of her fears as she saw no sign of Chica in the canyon.

"Well, I think we'd better get out of here," Uncle Biff said. "After all, there's no telling where our beak-nosed friend has gone or how soon he'll be back."

"I guess you're right," Linda agreed, moving towards the tie rail, her eyes on the ground. "But before you go, there's something I want you to see."

"What's that?" Uncle Biff asked.

"Bring the candle," Linda said. "I think we've got some proof."

"What is it?" Uncle Biff asked.

Linda took the candle and lowered it to the boot print that she'd found near the bucket. It wasn't as clear as the print in the barn had been, but she could see the notch and the clover leaf pattern in the heel.

"I hope you got a real good look at our captor," she said, "because this proves that he's your ghost and I think he's also the one who stole Mrs Barker's diamonds."

"You mean that's the same print?" Uncle Biff studied it with a frown.

"It matches the one we found in the barn and on the path to the ledge above the Inn, plus the partial print we found in Shadow Canyon," Linda confirmed.

Uncle Biff sighed. "Well, I can guarantee that I'll recognize him if I ever see him again, but I'll be darned if I can figure out what a man with a whole lot of very valuable diamonds would be doing holding us prisoner here or making trouble on a small ranch like Shadow Canyon."

"We'll ask him when we catch him," Linda said, fighting the pain in her head.

"Now we'd better get going. We've got a long, cold walk back to the ranch." Uncle Biff grinned at her. "I'm looking forward to it. Being out of that cave is wonderful." He led the way along the side of the canyon.

"Well, I—" Linda began, then stopped as her sharp ears caught the sound of hoofbeats.

"Someone's coming," Uncle Biff gasped.

Linda looked back, then ahead at the narrow entrance of the canyon. "And there's nowhere to hide!"

Fire 11

Linda, aware that they were too far from the cave, began running towards the canyon entrance. She'd only taken a few steps, however, when a white and gold horse came galloping around the rocks that guarded the entrance and skidded to a stop, whickering a greeting.

"Chica!" Linda cried, throwing her arms around the filly's sweat-damp neck, "you're safe."

"Linda? Linda, are you in there?" Bob's voice carried ahead of the three riders as they followed the filly into the narrow area.

"We're here," Uncle Biff answered for her, "and we're both safe—now."

"Uncle Biff?" Bob gasped. "What are you doing here? How did you find Linda? What . . . ?"

"Wait," Linda said. "We can talk while we ride. I don't think we should stay here any longer than we have to."

Bob nodded. "Why don't you hop up here behind me, Kathy," he suggested. "Let Uncle Biff take your horse. Linda, can you ride Chica without a bridle or saddle?"

Linda smiled wryly. "I rode her out here that way," she answered, then added a thank you as Uncle Biff helped her to mount the happy filly.

"Now tell us what happened," Larry said. "How did both of you get here? What is going on?"

Between them, Uncle Biff and Linda explained everything that had happened since his disappearance. Only then was Linda allowed to ask, "So how did you know where to find us? Why did you come?"

"Chica," the three chorused, making the filly start a little as she recognized her name.

"What do you mean?"

"She came galloping up to the house whinnying and carrying on like a crazy horse," Bob answered. "Woke us all up. That's when we discovered that you were missing."

"I couldn't believe it when I found your bed empty," Kathy added. "At first I thought that you were out with Chica, but when you weren't . . . Linda, we were scared to death. We didn't know what to do. Then Bob said that we should ask Chica where you were. She brought us here."

Bob laughed. "I'm glad we spent so much time playing hide-and-seek with her on the ranch, Sis. The moment I told her to go to you, she took off. We had a hard time keeping up with her."

Linda leaned forward to hug the filly again. "I was just so relieved that she got away," she admitted. "I really thought the ghost might have shot her. I was so worried."

"She's some horse!" Larry observed.

"Where's Wayne?" Uncle Biff asked, slowing his horse and looking around. "Why isn't he with you?"

Bob and Linda exchanged glances. "Good question," Bob said.

"Maybe he didn't hear you riding out," Linda suggested.

"Unless he was totally unconscious and buried

under about six feet of blankets, he would have heard Chica," Larry said. "I mean, can you believe a thousand-pound rooster crowing under your window?"

Everyone laughed, but the humour faded quickly and Linda finally asked the question she knew was on everyone's mind. "Uncle Biff, could Mr Upton be involved in all this?"

Uncle Biff shrugged. "I guess he could be, though I can't for the life of me think why he'd be doing it. He seemed genuinely interested in working for us and building up the reputation of the ranch. He's been good with the guests and . . . I just hate to think that I could be so wrong about a man. Why do you think he's involved?"

"Well, he did tell us that you drove off with two friends," Linda answered. "And he let someone take Chica."

"You didn't see him out there at the cave, did you?" Larry asked.

Uncle Biff shook his head. "The only person who came out there was Beak-nose. The other man was only with him when they flagged down my car."

"And Beak-nose is our ghost," Linda reminded them. "Not to mention the man on the ledge at the Furnace Creek Inn."

"Maybe hearing that will get the Sheriff started on a new investigation," Bob commented.

"At least it will give him another suspect to wonder about so he won't be so sure it was Andy."

"And there's a description of him," Linda added. "Uncle Biff got a good look at him."

"Hey, that's great. Maybe the police will even

have a picture of him that you can identify," Kathy suggested.

"That would help," Uncle Biff agreed. "I—"

Linda was looking towards the ranch and before Uncle Biff could go on, she squeezed her legs into Chica's sides. "Look," she shouted, "the ranch is on fire!"

The smoke that had caught her eye had become fingers of flame before they reached the stable yard. The horses in the corral were milling and whinnying with fear when Linda stopped Chica and slid off. The bunkhouse was blazing wildly and, as they watched, the door burst open and Wayne Upton came stumbling out.

"Quick, get some water," he shouted. "We've got to keep this from spreading. There's a hose attached to the barn faucet and one on the house, too."

For the next half hour they were all too busy to ask questions. The two streams of water wet down the roofs of the nearby buildings and then began to drown the flames, reducing them slowly to smouldering, steaming ruins.

Only then did they take time to catch their breath. Uncle Biff turned to Linda. "Why don't you put Chica in her stall, honey, and go and lie down," he said gently. "You don't look very well."

"Hey, you found your horse," Upton spoke up before Linda could reply. "I told you she just got loose, didn't I?"

"Didn't you hear Chica earlier?" Bob asked Upton. "She woke us up."

Upton yawned. "How long ago?" he asked without curiosity.

"About an hour, hour and a half," Larry said.

The bunkhouse was blazing wildly . .

Upton shrugged. "I wasn't here an hour ago," he stated. "I just got in about ten, fifteen minutes before you all came racing up. Good thing I did, too, or I wouldn't have seen him leaving."

"Seen who?" Biff asked.

"The ghost. He was just coming out of the bunkhouse when I came driving in. I tried to chase him, but he disappeared and . . . Well, I decided I'd better see what he was doing in the bunkhouse. That's when I found the fire. I tried to fight it, but . . ." He shrugged. "It was just too far along. I barely got out alive."

"You saw the ghost?" Linda asked, sceptical of what she was hearing.

Upton nodded. "I didn't believe in it before, but the way that thing just ran into the barn and disappeared . . ."

"Into the barn?" Bob's voice had an edge to it.

"That's right," Mr Upton replied. "I chased him into the barn and I figured I had him cornered. I closed the door and lit a lantern, but there was nobody there. I looked in every stall."

Linda tried to think, but her head ached too fiercely. "Come on, Chica," she said, putting an arm around the filly's neck to support herself. "Let's get you in your stall."

"Are you all right?" Bob asked, following her to the barn, where a lantern was still burning inside.

Linda sighed. "I don't know," she admitted as he fed the filly. "My head hurts from when I hit it. Do you believe Upton?" she asked, changing the subject.

Bob shrugged. "What he said is pretty much what happened to you the first night we were here, isn't it?"

Linda nodded, wincing. "I suppose it is," she

admitted. Then she picked up the lantern, carrying it to the rear of the barn.

The ground near the back wall was scuffed, but there were no boot prints that she could identify. Dizzy, she stumbled hard against the wall just at the spot where she'd found the original boot print. The click sounded loud in the quiet barn and the section of wall moved roughly a few inches to the right.

"What the heck . . . !" Bob gasped, coming to take her arm to steady her as they stared at the narrow opening that showed beside one of the old two-by-fours that supported each section of the wall.

Linda reached out one shaky hand and gave the board that she'd crashed into a tentative shove. It rolled aside silently, revealing a relatively small hollow on the other side.

"I think we've found our ghost's hideout," she murmured, shining the lantern light into the hollow, where it produced a glow from a discarded black hooded robe.

"Someone must have stacked all those hay bales just right to leave this space," Bob agreed. "And look at those boot prints. Just like all the others."

"The robe is kind of shiny," Linda observed.

Bob nodded. "Probably treated with some kind of luminous or reflector paint."

"I just wish our ghost was still in here," Linda said bitterly. "It seems like he's always one step ahead of us."

"I guess he must have slipped out while we were fighting the fire," Bob grumbled. "I sort of remember hearing hoofbeats, but I was too busy to check. I just assumed one of our horses was running away because of the fire."

Linda frowned. "This sort of proves Mr Upton's story, doesn't it?" she asked. "I mean about seeing the ghost run in here and disappear."

Bob nodded reluctantly. "Do you think Upton's innocent?" he asked. "I mean, he did lie about seeing Uncle Biff leave here with friends."

Linda straightened up, then staggered again, as her head still throbbed bitterly from the blow she'd received in the canyon. "I don't know what to think," she admitted, really ill, as the full effect of all that had happened washed over her.

"You go on up to the house and lie down," Bob ordered sternly, his eyes full of concern. "I'll finish taking care of Chica."

"But what about . . ." Linda waved a hand at the open panel.

"I'll tell Larry and Kathy and Uncle Biff about this. We'll stake it out for the rest of the night just in case our ghost decides to come back. Or maybe Mr Upton will come out to check on his ghost and we'll find out for sure whether he knows about this hideout or not." Bob's eyes were still tinged with suspicion.

Linda wanted to argue, but she was too sick and dizzy to even speak. But nodding agreement to his plan didn't help her head either, and she had to use most of her concentration to stay on her feet. As she passed Chica's stall, she gave the filly a light pat, then made her way towards the house.

It was dark now that the fire had burned down, and Linda had to fight a desire to simply lie down in the rough grass. It wasn't till she reached the kitchen door that she revived enough to realize that someone was talking inside the house. Curiosity overcame her pain for a moment and she moved past the kitchen door, following the side of the house to the open office window. There she stopped, recognizing Wayne Upton's voice.

"I know it's a mess, Al," he was saying, "but what did you expect?" There was a pause. "No, they're safe and I'll see they're delivered on time . . . Don't worry about my friend, he'll come through . . . I didn't make all the mistakes, you know. I'm just the one who has to keep covering them up . . . No, I can't tell you more now, just stay out of sight . . . You heard me. Now I've got to go. I'll call you when I get to Las Vegas."

Linda heard the sound of the receiver being replaced, and realizing that she couldn't allow Mr Upton to see her crouched near the house, she moved hurriedly away from the friendly wall, pulling her dark dressing gown tightly around her. The abrupt movements were too much for her already pounding head, however, and she stumbled, catching her foot in her dressing gown and falling heavily, bumping her head once again.

"Linda!" Kathy shouted just as Wayne Upton emerged from the house, stretching and yawning.

Linda struggled to sit up, trying to speak through the pain. She could feel Kathy's arm around her shoulders and she was dimly aware of her friend's anxious questions, but her main attention was on Upton as he headed for his car, which was parked right next to their horse trailer.

"Stop him," she gasped.

Kathy screamed for Mr Rogers, Bob, and Larry, but stayed with Linda as the three men surrounded Wayne Upton, backing him into the open horse trailer. Biff and Larry stood guard outside the trailer while Bob came running to Linda and Kathy.

"What happened?" Bob demanded. "Did he hurt you, Sis?"

"No," Linda answered weakly. "I just fell. He . . . he was on the phone. Strange call."

Bob frowned and Linda tried to come up with words of explanation, but her head hurt too much and the waves of dizziness came sweeping over her. "Take her in and put her to bed, Kathy," Bob ordered.

"We'll search Upton and his car, make sure that he isn't up to something."

Linda tried to protest that she wanted to question the man, but no words came, and in a moment she was inside on her bed, shivering with reaction to her wild adventures. Kathy wrapped her tightly in an extra quilt, then brought her warm milk. Linda tried to stay awake, but it was no use. Her eyes closed and she was asleep.

It was bright daylight when she opened her eyes again. Kathy's bed was already made and the air was sweet with the scents of ham and eggs and freshly baked muffins. Linda sat up carefully, memories of last night's headache fresh in her mind; but apart from a tender lump, her head felt fine. She jumped out of bed, washed and dressed quickly, eager to join the others in the kitchen.

"I told you the smell of food would bring her out," Bob crowed as she emerged. "How do you feel? Are you all right?"

"I'm starving," Linda answered, with a grin. "How about the rest of you? Uncle Biff?"

"Are you sure you're all right?" Uncle Biff asked. "You were really out of it last night. You could have a concussion."

"My head feels fine," Linda assured him, then sobered as she remembered what had happened just before Kathy had forced her into bed. "What happened to Mr Upton?"

Uncle Biff sighed. "He's gone. He quit. Left right after we searched him and his car. What was that all about, anyway? Did you think he'd taken something from the house, or what?"

Linda explained quickly about the phone call, doing her best to remember all that had been said. "I wanted to ask him some questions, but . . ." She sighed, then shrugged.

"We'll see if we can find him in Las Vegas," Uncle Biff told her.

"Las Vegas?" Linda was surprised.

Uncle Biff laughed. "I called Elaine first thing this morning and she suggested that we'd better get there. Mr Pendleton is out of the hospital at last, so she'll be free to join us. Did you forget that you're due to ride in a horse show tomorrow afternoon?"

Linda swallowed hard, then grinned. "As a matter of fact, I did," she admitted.

"Do you feel well enough?" Bob asked. "You were pretty weird last night, Sis."

"All I need is breakfast," Linda assured them, sinking down and attacking the food that was passed to her. After several bites, she asked, "What about the ghost? Did he come back last night?"

Larry and Bob shook their heads. "We hid in an empty stall and waited, but there wasn't any sign of him."

"I don't think he'll be back," Uncle Biff said.

"What do you mean?" Linda asked.

"The phone call you overheard seems to prove that Upton was working with our ghost. I expect Beak-nose is the man he said he'd call in Vegas."

"Oh, no!" Linda wailed.

"What's the matter?" Kathy asked.

"If Beak-nose has the diamonds, how will we ever find them?" Linda asked, her eyes meeting her brother's and reading his understanding.

"We have to find those diamonds if we're going to clear Andy," Bob reminded them all bleakly.

Uncle Biff nodded grimly. "I called the Sheriff's office last night and told him about the kidnapping and the boot prints. I gave him the man's description."

"What did he say?" Linda asked, trying to hope.

"That he'd look into it, but that there was really nothing beside your theory to link the two crimes. I don't think he really believes that our kidnapper is his diamond thief."

"We have to do something," Linda muttered, eating mechanically now that her thoughts were all focused on Las Vegas and what they might find there.

"We'll do our best," Uncle Biff promised, but she sensed that he didn't have much hope of helping poor Andy.

Old Friends 12

The rest of the morning was spent preparing for the trip to Las Vegas. Biff Rogers had to call in a neighbour to stay at the ranch and take care of the stock since Wayne Upton had quit and, of course, everyone had to pack.

Linda, however, was more concerned about Chica, taking her out into the corral and riding her around for a few minutes to make sure that her night's adventures hadn't left her with any stiffness or injuries. Luckily, aside from the chafe marks of the hobbles, she was sound and eager. Laughing, Linda took the time to put the filly through her entire repertoire of tricks.

"She's in terrific shape," Uncle Biff called, coming to watch from the corral fence. "You're going to be the hit of the horse show."

"You wouldn't be prejudiced, would you?" Linda teased.

"Because she helped free us, don't be silly." Uncle Biff laughed with her. Then he grew more sober. "Do you think the trouble here is over, Linda?" he asked. "I mean now that Upton is gone and we've discovered the hiding place in the barn, do you think they'll leave Shadow Canyon Guest Ranch alone?"

Linda could only shrug. "I guess we won't be sure till we know why they were doing it in the first place," she admitted. "And we can't find that out till they are caught . . . if we can catch them."

"If I ever get my hands on Beak-nose, I'll make sure he tells us," Uncle Biff grated. "After what he tried to do to both of us . . ."

"I think we should just be grateful for Chica's intelligence," Linda soothed him. "She's the one thing they didn't count on."

"Your secret weapon," Uncle Biff agreed, then laughed as Chica reached out and neatly stole the handkerchief out of his back pocket. The filly raced across the corral, waving the handkerchief like a flag. Uncle Biff chuckled. "You can have it, Chica," he called. "You've earned it."

The filly snorted, then came trotting back, dropping the handkerchief at his feet. Uncle Biff rewarded her with a piece of the apple he'd been eating.

"Are we going to be staying at the motel with Aunt Elaine and the Pendletons?" Linda asked as she followed Uncle Biff out of the corral, leaving Chica to enjoy her freedom a little longer before she had to be loaded into the horse trailer for the trip to Las Vegas.

"I don't think so," he answered. "Elaine says that the Kingsleys have invited all of us to stay with them till after the show."

"Kingsleys?" Linda frowned. "That name rings a bell."

Uncle Biff laughed. "I don't know how you could remember," he said. "You weren't much more than six or seven when we took you to see their horses."

"Kingsley Arabians?" Linda gasped.

"You do remember?"

She nodded. "Are you joking? That was one of the happiest days of my life! I fell in love with one of their horses and Mr Kingsley led him all around the area while I rode him. I made everyone's life miserable for months afterwards because I wanted to go back and see that horse again."

"That was their prize stallion El Sirocco. You'll be able to see him while we're there."

"You mean the horse show is at the Kingsley Arabian Ranch?" Linda was unable to believe her ears.

Uncle Biff nodded. "I expect they'll be interested in seeing Chica d'Oro, too," he said. "She's Half-Arabian, isn't she?"

Linda nodded. "Her dam was Ranashi. I think she was from Nevada, so they might know something about her."

"If it wasn't for her colour, I'd think she was a purebred Arabian," Uncle Biff commented. "Who was her sire?"

"A palomino Saddlebred, Golden Supreme."

"You'll have to tell Van and Paula Kingsley all about how you happened to get Chica," Uncle Biff told her. "They may even have some of her relatives on their ranch."

"Oh, how exciting," Linda gasped. "I'd love to know more about her background. I know I was lucky to be able to register her at all, considering the way she came to me. But I've always been curious about her ancestors. She's such a special horse."

"So let's go see if everybody else is ready to go," Uncle Biff suggested. "We have nearly a hundred miles to drive and I'm pretty anxious to see that wife of mine."

"I'll bet she'll be glad to see you, too," Linda observed. "She was terribly worried about you."

The drive to the Kingsley Ranch was uneventful, but when they drove into the wide, raked-gravel parking area, Uncle Biff sat forward. "That's our car," he shouted. "Elaine must be here!"

The carved double doors of the main house opened even as he spoke, and in a moment Aunt Elaine was hugging all of them. It was several minutes before Linda looked up to see the older couple, who were introduced as the Kingsleys, Van and Paula.

"I think perhaps you're truly responsible for my love of horses," Linda confided shyly as the Kingsleys welcomed them. "I never forgot my wonderful visit to your ranch."

"Wait till you see her filly," Uncle Biff said. "She's a real beauty."

"Why don't I guide you to the stable area now," Mr Kingsley suggested. "Your horses must be tired of riding in the trailer and their stalls are ready."

"Let's get them settled quickly," Paula Kingsley said. "We're very eager to hear more about the adventures you've been having. Elaine has just told us the bare facts of all you've been through."

The huge stable complex of the Kingsley Ranch was beautifully cared for, and Linda gasped with delight at the horses she saw in the small paddocks. "Can you imagine having so many horses to choose from?" she murmured. "I'd never have time for them all. I'm glad I have just one Chica to worry about."

"Considering the things that have happened to you, one horse is enough," Larry teased.

They were directed to a very attractive stable building near the big main house. "The two end stalls are yours," Mr Kingsley informed them. "As soon as you've unloaded your horses, one of the grooms will drive your trailer to our parking garage. That way you won't have to worry about it."

"Our tack is stored in the front compartment of the trailer," Bob told him.

"You can unload it and put it in our tack room or you can leave it in the trailer," Paula Kingsley assured him. "It will be safe either place. We have a good security force working here, especially with the show set for tomorrow."

Mr Kingsley moved to the rear of the horse trailer. "Enough talk," he announced. "I want to see the wonder horse."

Paula laughed. "Easy to see where his interests are," she teased as the others joined in her laughter.

Bob unhooked and lowered the ramp while Linda moved to the side of the trailer. "Back, Chica. Back, Rocket," she ordered, sure that the two well-travelled horses would respond as they always did by backing out of the trailer stalls.

Rocket moved out at once, stepping carefully down the ramp, then standing while Bob snapped a leadrope on his halter. Chica, however, merely stamped her feet and snorted, then began pawing at the floor beneath the small manger.

"Has she got her halter caught or something?" Bob asked as Linda climbed into Rocket's side of the trailer and hurried forward, her eyes expertly checking the filly for signs of distress.

"I don't see anything," she answered as she reached across the low barricade and snapped her leadrope on Chica's halter. "Back, Chica," she ordered more sternly.

The filly took a step, then pawed again at the front wall of the trailer. "Back," Linda ordered again. The filly obeyed, snorting slightly, then dancing as her hooves touched solid ground. Linda quickly led her in a small circle to make sure that her pawing hadn't been a sign of discomfort in her legs and hooves.

She was still studying Chica when Mr Kingsley stepped forward, his face unreadable. "Where did you get that filly?" he demanded. "What is her breeding?"

Linda gulped slightly. "She's Arabian and Saddlebred. Her mother was an Arabian mare named Ranashi and her father was Golden Supreme."

"Ranashi." Mr Kingsley's voice was full of sadness. "I knew it. Except for the colour, she could be Ranashi the way she was when I first saw her."

"You knew Ranashi?" Linda asked, remembering the tragic story of the mare, stolen and so badly injured that she'd died shortly after giving birth to Chica.

"My dear girl, El Sirocco was Ranashi's sire," Mr Kingsley answered.

"Your stallion is Chica's grandfather?" Linda gasped, unable to believe what she was hearing.

"There's no doubt about it," Mr Kingsley said. "Even if you hadn't known her mother's name, I would have recognized the blood. You have a prize-winning Half-Arabian there, Linda. Have you entered her in any Arabian shows?"

Linda shook her head. "I've been showing her mostly in Parade Classes or the Trail Class."

"With her colour and intelligence, I can understand that, but I think you'd do well in halter classes in the Arabian shows. There are a lot of them out in California, you know." He smiled. "In fact, you might even make her an added entry in the

Half-Arabian fillies at our show. I'd be proud to have her competing."

"If you'll tell me what I have to do, I'd be happy to try," Linda said shyly, then laughed as Chica danced around her, arching her neck and switching her thick white tail. "And, as you can see, Chica d'Oro loves to show off."

"There's a practice class this evening. You can try it then," he informed her. "Now, however, let's get the horses stabled so you can tell us all about your adventures at Shadow Canyon Guest Ranch. According to Elaine, you and your filly have been most heroic."

The recounting of Chica's story and the tale of their brush with the human ghost on the dude ranch provided plenty of conversation through the leisurely dinner at the Kingsleys' long, handsomely set table. Even the Pendletons, who had joined them, were impressed. There was no time for Linda to wonder about Chica's strange behaviour in the trailer or to speculate on the filly's seeming reluctance to set her hooves on the ranch where so many of her mother's relatives lived.

After dinner, Chica and Linda joined a half-dozen horses and trainers in the lighted practice ring under Mr Kingsley's watchful eye. From his instructions, she quickly learned how to show the filly at an animated walk and a showy trot as well as how to stand the filly to reveal her excellent conformation.

It was different to show the filly from the ground instead of riding her, Linda decided. Chica seemed to enjoy it, however, posing obediently, her golden coat rippling under the lights, her silvery mane and tail flowing in perfect contrast.

Only after the class when she returned the filly to her stall and to Mike, the stableman who was in charge of the building where Chica and Rocket were being kept, did her happy mood fade. "Did you call Andy?" she asked Bob.

He nodded, his expression making it clear that he'd heard nothing good.

"How is he?" she inquired.

Bob shrugged. "I think he's given up," he said sadly. "He sounded like he didn't have any hope even when I told him that the boot prints proved our ghost was the man at Furnace Creek. He said it didn't matter since someone put that money in his bank account. Even the lawyer thinks that makes him look guilty."

"We have to do something," Linda groaned.

"Tomorrow, after the horse show," Larry soothed her. "Biff says we're invited to spend another night here, and the Kingsleys have invited the Pendletons, too. We'll all go into town tomorrow night, so maybe we can look around for Upton and Beak-nose then."

"We have to find them," Linda said with a sigh. "Finding them and talking to them is the only way we'll ever be able to help Andy."

Horse Show Honours 13

The morning of the horse show began well as they all sat down to huge platters of waffles, ham, eggs, and fresh fruit. Mr Kingsley smiled at Linda. "How are you feeling today, Linda?" he asked. "Ready to face the judges? Halter classes are always held in the morning so that the afternoon is left free for performance classes."

Linda groaned. "I just hope I don't make any mistakes that will cost Chica points. I want so much for you to be proud of us." Her smile included Uncle Biff and Aunt Elaine. "After all, we're representing the Shadow Canyon Guest Ranch today."

"Don't worry a minute," Mr Kingsley assured her. "In fact, I'll have a little surprise for you this afternoon at the end of the show. A surprise for you and Chica."

Linda opened her mouth to ask him what he was talking about, but his expression stopped her and she returned her attention to her plate. Though she was too nervous to be hungry, she finished her breakfast to fill the hollowness she felt and then excused herself to go up to change.

For the halter class, Linda chose to wear the same burgundy western suit that she'd worn on the first trip to Death Valley. It gave her confidence to know that she at least looked as professional as the other trainers who were leading in their lovely fillies.

It was a fairly large class, with an interesting variety of horses. Linda and Chica took their place in the line about mid-way in the group. They all circled the arena once at a showy walk, then stopped while the judges considered each entry individually as they were led forward at a walk, posed, and then led away from the judges at an animated trot.

Linda studied the other horses. With her well-trained eye, she quickly eliminated a pretty bay with calf knees and a lively grey whose shoulder was much too upright for proper stride. The others were not as easy to fault and she saw several that were almost as well-balanced and had nearly as perfect legs as Chica.

The judges gave each entry full attention, marking on their clipboards. Linda's heart nearly stopped when she was signalled forward, but she swallowed hard and led the excited, dancing filly towards the judges.

"Stand, Chica," she ordered and was pleased that the filly stood proudly, her delicate head high, her nostrils flaring, her large dark eyes bright with interest. The breeze blew her silvery mane around and combed through her tail.

The judges walked around them both, then waved Linda to move on. Linda ran so that Chica would trot her best, showing her strong stride and the elegant way she lifted her small hooves. Then it was over and they were back standing along the rail waiting while the other horses made their appearance before the judges.

"Smile and keep Chica alert," a friendly voice advised from the other side of the arena rail. Linda turned to see Mike, the stableman, standing there.

Linda led Chica before the judges . . .

"Well, hi," she greeted him. "Do you think we did all right?"

"You looked great," he assured her, "but don't look worried now. The judges watch the horses on the rail, too, and they'll think they missed some fault in your filly if you appear too concerned."

Linda laughed. "Thank you for grooming her this morning," she continued. "I would never have had time to polish her hooves and everything else, too. And the show halter is beautiful."

"Mr Kingsley wanted her to look her best—and she does." Mike grinned. "She's a real special filly."

"Thank you. She's—" Linda stopped as the announcer's voice crackled over the sound system and began calling numbers. Her heart skipped as she heard hers. The remaining horses were dismissed, and she and the other five selected horses moved to the middle of the arena where Chica stood obediently as the judges studied and compared the finalists one last time.

Linda held her breath as the numbers were announced once again, this time starting with the sixth place ribbon and moving with agonizing slowness towards the blue ribbon. Finally, only a handsome black filly and Chica remained, and it was forever before the second place number was called—the black filly's number.

Applause and shouts from the crowd greeted the announcement that Chica d'Oro was the winner, and Chica trotted out to accept her ribbon like the seasoned show horse she was. Never had Linda been more proud of her golden filly.

"Well, I guess now you'll want to enter more

halter classes," Bob said when he, Larry, and Kathy met her at the exit gate.

Linda grinned at him, then nodded. "It's good to have other people think she's as perfect as I do. And she is, you know—that win proves it."

"So now all you have to do is prove that she is as well-trained as she is gorgeous," Larry observed. "Winning the Parade Class should do that."

Linda sighed. "I'm not so sure we can do that," she admitted. "There are some pretty terrific horses entered and all of them are a lot older than Chica, which means they are much more experienced."

"You'll be riding the smartest horse here," Kathy reminded her loyally. "So don't worry."

"Would you like me to take Chica back to her stall for you so you can watch the rest of the halter classes?" Mike asked, coming to join them. "Chica's half-brother will be in purebred stallions, six and older. Rahsheed."

The classes passed quickly and, with the aid of a programme, Linda soon identified several more of Ranashi's sons and daughters. Looking at them, she came to realize even more how much Chica must resemble her mother. Except for her golden coat and silver mane, Chica was very much like the other horses.

Lunch was a delicious barbecue cooked in a deep pit that had been dug a short distance from the arena. Then, after visiting with the Pendletons, who were enjoying the horse show, and being introduced to several other groups of friends that had come to see Uncle Biff and Aunt Elaine, it was time for Linda to go change for the Parade Class.

Dressed in her beautiful green and white embroidered parade outfit, Linda felt her confidence returning. Chica was the prettiest horse on the ranch, she told herself firmly, and she was perfectly trained, so why shouldn't they do well in the class?

The Parade Class was scheduled near the end of the show and as Linda took her place in the line of horses, she gasped in shock. This was certainly to be no ordinary contest, she realized even before the announcer began to explain the rules.

"Since this is a class open to all breeds, we have decided to make the event more interesting by testing the horses and riders with real parade conditions. In the judging, half the points will be determined by the appearance of the horse, rider, and equipment. The other half will be determined by the way the horse behaves under the conditions of the class."

There was a muttering among several of the contestants, but everyone rode into the arena when the gate was opened. Linda looked at the fifteen other riders and took a deep breath.

About half of them were in Arabian garb or costume, the outfits varying from desert sheiks to harem girls and the horses were almost completely covered by all manner of beautiful material, pompoms, fringes, and tassels. The rest of the contestants, like Linda, rode with western equipment ranging from a beautiful white saddle on a tall black stallion to several silver-mounted saddles that looked like they weighed a ton.

Linda patted Chica's shoulder, then urged her forward at her animated trot as they all circled the arena. The first circuit was uneventful, but after that, things changed and Linda began to realize what the announcer had meant.

Hidden loud speakers suddenly erupted with the sounds of firecrackers; flags were carried in by the ring attendants and handed to the riders to hold for a moment. Loud music blared and faded, then blared again at odd moments as they walked, trotted, and cantered around the arena.

Several of the highly-strung horses, conditioned more to the showring than to the hazards of a real parade, reacted badly and were dismissed; but Chica accepted all the surprises without a bit of panic. Linda's comforting hand on her shoulder and her whispered, "That's my good girl," were all that was necessary.

The class seemed to go on forever and, with each new explosion of sound, Linda felt herself growing more tense, more afraid of making a mistake. Still, Chica moved with pride and confidence, her trust in Linda so complete that not even a flag snapping about her ears frightened her.

"Line up, please. Line up," came the order, and Linda rode to the centre of the arena with the nine other riders, who were all that remained of the sixteen who'd started the class.

The judges studied them all again, walking around to view each horse from all sides, then asking that the horse be backed up. Chica was flawless, arching her neck and tail and standing like a statue. Linda smiled with pride in the filly.

Once again the numbers were called, and as they moved nearer to the blue, Linda felt her hands go cold. What if she hadn't been placed? As the entry from Shadow Canyon Guest Ranch, she'd hoped to gain some publicity for her friends, but if she was dismissed without a ribbon . . .

Her number was called. "First prize to the Shadow Canyon Guest Ranch entry, Chica d'Oro, owned and ridden by Linda Craig. Congratulations, Linda."

Linda rode forward, then signalled Chica to bow, first to the audience, who cheered wildly, then to the judges, who smiled in surprise and pleasure. The blue ribbon was pinned to Chica's bridle and Linda accepted the handsome parade trophy with thanks.

Once again Mike was waiting at the gate. "Let me take Chica," he said. "You stay here and watch the next class, and then it will be time for the parade of stallions, the grand finale of the show."

"Will El Sirocco be in the Parade?" Linda asked.

Mike nodded. "As the oldest stallion here, he'll lead it and he'll be honoured by having some of his finest sons and daughters shown with him as a tribute to his fine bloodlines."

The final class seemed endless, but once the ribbons and trophy were awarded, Linda moved closer to the rail near the arena gate, anxious to see the stallions that were waiting to be led in for the final parade. Suddenly her name was called and she turned to find that Mike was standing in the line of horses and he was holding Chica's leadline.

Frowning, Linda hurried over to him. "What is she doing here?" she asked, noticing that Chica was freshly groomed and that her two blue ribbons had been pinned one to each side of the show halter.

"My idea," Mr Kingsley said, leading the handsome old stallion over. "I know that Chica is only a Half-Arabian, but she epitomizes the very best of the Arabian tradition of horses' serving and loving people, so I've asked that she be included in the parade of Sirocco's offspring. I've given the announcer the story of all she has done this past week, including her rescue of you and Biff Rogers. I hope you don't mind the surprise."

Linda met his gaze with shining eyes. "Mind?" she gasped. "We'd be honoured to be in such royal company."

"Then let's go." Mr Kingsley led the way into the arena, El Sirocco dancing and half-rearing like a colt in spite of his twenty-four years. A half-dozen beautiful stallions, mares, and colts followed him. Then the announcer called Chica's name and began telling the story of her adventures while Linda led the prancing palomino around to a well-deserved round of applause. Never had Linda been more proud of her horse or the fine tradition she represented. It was, she decided, the most wonderful horse show she'd ever been in!

The glow stayed with Linda all the way to the stable as people crowded around to ask about Chica and to congratulate her on her blue ribbons. However, once she was alone in the quiet stall, her happiness faded, for she remembered that tonight they must try to find Wayne Upton and Beak-nose. Tonight might be their very last chance to help rescue Andy from the horrible accusations against him.

Unexpected Wrangler 14

Linda had little time to worry about what lay ahead as Kathy, Larry, and Bob joined her at the stable, adding their congratulations to those she had already received.

"Ready for tonight?" Bob asked. "Mr Pendleton just told us that he has tickets for all of us to attend a dinner show at one of the big downtown hotels. It's his way of thanking Aunt Elaine for staying in Las Vegas with Sylvia and Jimmy, he said."

"Wow," Linda gasped, "that sounds like fun. What kind of a show is it?"

"A musical," Bob answered. "It's supposed to be very good."

"We'd better go to the house and get changed," Linda said, her spirits reviving at the prospect of a new adventure. She grinned at Kathy. "It will seem strange to wear a dress, won't it?"

Kathy giggled. "Sometimes I forget there are such things. I just automatically reach for my riding clothes."

"We probably won't recognize either one of you," Larry teased, then winked at Linda.

"Just so you don't leave us behind," she told him.

"We will if you don't hurry," Bob warned. "Everyone wants to walk around downtown a little before we go to the Union Plaza for the show."

"What are you going to wear?" Linda asked Kathy

when they reached their room in the Kingsley house.

"I really don't have much choice," Kathy confided as she opened the closet and took out a rose pink dress of a soft knit material. "This has a fancy silver belt and with my silver snowflake necklace it should look dressy. What about you?"

Linda lifted a simple turquoise dress from its hanger. The style and lines were very plain, but the neckline was trimmed with delicate gold embroidery. She added a jacket of soft, sheer turquoise material that was shot through with golden threads that caught the light when she moved.

"Wow," Kathy gasped. "I've seen the dress before, but that jacket is super."

"It was a gift from my grandmother," Linda explained. "She said that she thought I'd need something dressy for the holidays and tonight should be a good time to try it out."

"We're going to make a pretty classy pair," Kathy told her as they both turned their attention to combing the wind-tangles and arena dust from their hair.

As she brushed her honey-coloured hair, Kathy's face became solemn. "I did find out something today," she said.

"What's that?" Linda asked.

"Well, I sat with the Pendletons while you were in the horse show and I told them about the tripwire that set off the landslide in the canyon."

"What did they say?" Linda asked, her attention immediately caught.

"Neither Jimmy nor Mr Pendleton remembered hitting anything. In fact, they weren't even on their horses when the slide started. They were climbing up the side of the canyon."

"So what do you think happened?" Linda asked, aware from Kathy's guarded expression that there was more.

"Sylvia said that she was holding the horses, so she didn't move, but Mr Upton did. She told me that he rode forward just about the time the slide started."

"So he set it off," Linda observed.

"By accident or on purpose?" Kathy asked, her tone making it clear that she really didn't expect an answer.

Linda shrugged. "If we find him tonight, maybe we can ask him," she murmured.

A tap on the door ended the conversation and Aunt Elaine came in to say, "I think we'd better be on our way pretty soon, girls. We only have about an hour to wander in the downtown souvenir shops before the show."

"We're ready," Linda said, picking up her little gold evening purse and looking at Kathy, "aren't we?"

The downtown area was well-lit in the early darkness of the winter afternoon, and there were plenty of other people crowding the sidewalks between the seemingly endless lines of shops and clubs, hotels, and restaurants. Linda looked around and shook her head. "It's pretty and exciting, I guess, but I really like the horse ranch better."

Everyone laughed. "Somehow, that doesn't surprise me," Bob told her.

"You'll love the play," Aunt Elaine promised.

"I'm sure I will," Linda answered, "and this has been a fantastic day. I guess I just can't stop thinking about Andy. I feel so helpless. Nothing we have done has helped him."

Uncle Biff sighed. "Well, we'll spend tomorrow talking to the Las Vegas police, if you like. Even though Andy was arrested in California, maybe we can learn something. And, of course, we do have the kidnapping charges against Beak-nose and his friend. There's always a chance I'll be able to recognize one or the other of them from a police photograph. They were definitely criminal types. I'd have gone in sooner, but there just hasn't been time since we arrived."

"Thanks, Uncle Biff," Bob and Linda chorused as they walked on along the street towards the big hotel.

When they stopped on the corner across the street from the hotel to wait for the light to change, Linda looked back the way they'd come, and as she did so, a familiar figure caught her eye. She stood on tiptoe, straining to see into the shadows beneath the neon signs.

"Hey, look, there's the list of the stars in the play," Bob shouted above the sounds of the traffic and the jovial crowd.

Linda glanced around, startled, and when she turned back the figure she'd been watching had vanished. She continued to stare over her shoulder till Larry took her arm. "Hey, come on, what is so interesting back there?" he asked. "The play is across the street."

Linda frowned at the seething crowd. "For a minute, I thought I saw Wayne Upton over there."

"What?" Biff turned to her at once.

Linda described what she'd seen, including the rather distinctive suede and lamb's wool jacket she'd seen the wrangler wearing on the cold mornings at the ranch. "But I must have been mistaken," she finished. "I mean, he didn't have the jacket when we put out the fire, so it probably burned up in the bunkhouse. He said he lost everything, didn't he?"

"It was in his car," Uncle Biff corrected. "I saw it when we searched it." He looked at his watch. "I think I'll go take a look around for him," he said. "Why don't all of you go ahead and get in the queue for the play. I'll join you in a few minutes. All right?"

They agreed reluctantly and crossed the street to enter the busy hotel. The crowd inside was even larger than the one on the sidewalk and it took them several minutes to find the queue that was waiting outside the red-draped entrance to the showroom. Once there, however, there was little to do but wait. The queue was just beginning to move when Biff Rogers came hurrying through the crowd to join them.

"Did you see him?" Linda asked before anyone else could speak.

Uncle Biff shook his head. "That's a big crowd out there. I must have missed him."

"I could have been wrong," Linda admitted. "I want so badly to find Mr Upton. He is our best hope for catching Beak-nose and I did hear him say he was coming to Las Vegas."

"We all do, honey," Uncle Biff said, "and we'll try again tomorrow."

"Now, however, let's go see a nice happy musical," Aunt Elaine suggested. "We can forget all our troubles for a few hours. All right?"

Linda tossed her dark hair and smoothed the turquoise and gold jacket. "Sounds good to me," she said as they stepped through the doorway and into the theatre. Though she knew Andy's plight would not be far from her thoughts, there was nothing more she could do at the moment. She only hoped that they'd be able to find Wayne Upton again and that their suspicions were correct in connecting him to the ghostly Beak-nose.

The theatre was lovely, effectively banishing the noisy room they'd left with the elegance of deep carpeting, crystal chandeliers, and quiet dignity. They were led to a table for ten on one of the four tiers of tables that formed a half-circle around the stage.

Dinner proved to be excellent and when the curtains opened, the play was all that had been promised. The cast was young and full of excitement, singing well and dancing with fire and skill. Linda was so totally caught up in it that it was several minutes after the grand finale before she fully returned to her surroundings.

"Oh, it must be wonderful to be in something like that," Kathy sighed. "To wear those gorgeous costumes and be able to sing and dance and act and . . ."

"It's like a dream," Linda agreed, smiling sleepily as she followed Elaine through the exciting crowd.

The floating feeling stayed with Linda till they all reached the cool air of the night world beyond the hotel, and then she blinked and looked around. Almost at once her eyes were drawn to a familiar figure.

Linda stiffened and reached out to clutch Aunt Elaine's arm, wishing desperately that Uncle Biff, Larry, and Bob hadn't already left them to go get the two cars that would be required to drive them all back to Kingsley Ranch. "It's them!" she gasped.

"That must be Beak-nose—and he's with Mr Upton!"

At the sound of her voice, Wayne Upton turned and for just a heartbeat their eyes met. He then spun around and the three men started to run. Without stopping to think, Linda plunged into the crowd after them.

It was like running through molasses as she pushed and dodged her way between people and she soon lost sight of everyone but Wayne Upton. His distinctive jacket was easy to follow and she pursued it with all her strength.

The crowd thinned a little and Linda slowed, trying to spot the other men. Suddenly strong hands struck her from behind, pushing her violently towards the street and the rushing late-evening traffic. Terrified, Linda screamed and grabbed frantically at a street sign, barely stopping herself in time to avoid getting hit by a car. Shaking, she clung to the cold metal, gasping for breath.

"Linda, Linda, are you all right?" Aunt Elaine, Kathy, and the Pendletons came racing to her side.

"They got away," Linda panted, frustration bringing tears to her eyes. "Someone pushed me towards the street and while I was catching my balance, they just disappeared."

"We'll catch them again," Aunt Elaine soothed her. "Now come on back to the front of the hotel. Biff and the boys will be waiting for us."

Though she longed to argue, Linda went obediently and did her best to explain just what had happened when she and Kathy joined Larry and Bob in their car while Aunt Elaine and the Pendletons joined Uncle Biff in the other car. "If only I could have caught them," Linda finished.

"Well, we know one thing for sure now," Larry said. "They're all in it together. Plus, you, at least, have seen Beak-nose and the other man."

"I think I'd recognize them," Linda acknowledged, "but what good will that do for Andy? All we know for sure about them is that they haunted the ranch. We have to catch them and make them confess to stealing the diamonds or Andy will never be free."

Bob, Kathy, and Larry all looked as though they'd like to argue. But there was nothing they could say and, because of that, they rode all the way back to Kingsley Ranch in tired, unhappy silence.

"They probably already sold the diamonds and were out spending the money tonight," Linda observed bitterly as they made a quick circle by the stable to check on Rocket and Chica before going to bed.

"Uncle Biff can charge Beak-nose and his friends with kidnapping," Bob reminded her.

"How will that help Andy?" Linda asked.

Bob shrugged, unable to answer.

"Be glad we're staying here and not at some motel," Larry said, changing the subject. "At least the Kingsleys have plenty of security. Guard dogs, grooms in every stable building—it's great. No way they could have a resident ghost."

Linda managed a weak smile, but as they made their way upstairs to their rooms, she couldn't shake the feeling that she'd failed Andy. Upton and his friends had only to leave Las Vegas and they'd never be able to find them again.

The feeling of unrest was still with Linda as she slipped between the cool sheets and closed her eyes. She was very tired, but her mind gave her no rest.

She'd barely dropped into a light doze when the barking of the dogs woke her. Night sounds came from beyond the open window. Stable noises, the night wind stirring the palms, a sleepy bird protesting—then a horse's whinny, loud and urgent. Chica's whinny!

Linda slipped out of bed and pulled on her trainers and dressing gown, shivering at the memory of what had happened the last time she'd heard Chica in the night. But this was another ranch, she reminded herself and there were other people close by. She let herself out into the hall and was padding towards the stairs when a door opened and Uncle Biff stepped out.

"Where are you going?" he whispered.

"The dogs woke me and I heard a horse . . . Chica, I think."

Uncle Biff nodded. "We'll go and check it out."

The night was breezy and cold and the land was shadowed as they hurried across the open sections, heading for the long ranks of stable buildings. They were halfway there when they heard the solid crash of hooves hitting a stall door, quickly followed by Chica's squeal of rage. Linda started to run, stumbling on the uneven footing, too frightened to wait.

"That's the right horse, all right," Wayne Upton's voice carried clearly on the night air, stopping her in her tracks. "You can tell by the way she reacts to Al."

"If it wasn't for the noise she's making, I'd give her something to remember me by," the man called Al snarled. "Too bad I didn't hit her when I took a shot at her in the canyon."

"It'd be an awful waste," a third voice remarked. "If you hadn't let her get loose, we could have picked up some cash selling her."

"Now that we've found the horses, what do we do?" Wayne asked.

"How should I know?" Al snapped. "You got us into this mess, so—"

Before he could go on, two large dark shapes hurtled past Linda and Biff and rounded the corner where they'd taken refuge. The snarling guard dogs hit Beak-nose and Wayne in the chest, knocking them to the ground, then turned to menace the third man, who backed against the stable building, his hands over his head.

"Don't move or they will attack," a man's voice ordered, and Mike came out of the stable tack room. "Hold, King. Shah, guard!"

The two Dobermans stepped back, their eyes on the three men, their mouths open enough to display their sharp white fangs. Mike stood behind them, smiling. "I've called the police," he informed the men. "There's a patrol car on the way, so we'll soon find out what you're doing on the Kingsleys' land."

"They were here looking for Chica," Linda said, stepping out into the light that reflected from the tack room doorway.

"You know these men?" Mike asked, looking from her to Biff Rogers and back again.

"We've met," Uncle Biff answered, "but they aren't friends. In fact, they kidnapped me and they held Linda captive. We also have reason to believe that they stole some very valuable diamonds from a lady at the Furnace Creek Inn in Death Valley."

"Diamonds? Us? We don't have any diamonds." Wayne smiled, then sobered as he heard the wail of a siren. In a moment a patrol car came screeching towards them.

Uncle Biff took Linda's arm gently. "You don't need to stay here, honey," he told her. "I'm the one who can identify our friends, so they don't need you. I'll make sure everything is investigated, believe me."

Linda wanted to object, but a whicker from the nearby stall drew her to Chica's side. She slipped into the warm darkness of the stall and stood stroking the filly till Uncle Biff came to lean over the stall door.

"I'm going into the city with them," he told her. "Tell Elaine and the Kingsleys, please. I'll call as soon as I know anything."

"Let's just hope you have some good news," Linda told him.

"Keep your fingers crossed," he said. "At least we've got them now."

Linda nodded, though she knew he couldn't see her in the dark stall. In spite of his words, she had a dreadful feeling that it wasn't over yet.

Aunt Elaine was waiting in the brightly lit kitchen of the big house when Linda returned. "I heard the siren," she said. "What's going on?"

Linda explained quickly about hearing Chica and the capture of the three men. Elaine listened intently, then laughed with delight. "Then it's all over," she shouted.

Linda said nothing.

"What's wrong, Linda?" Aunt Elaine asked, sobering. "They've caught the men, isn't that what you wanted?"

Linda nodded, but she couldn't summon up the relief that Aunt Elaine seemed to be feeling. They might have caught the ghost, but what about the diamonds?

Van and Paula Kingsley came in to join them and, after a few moments, they were all settled around the kitchen table with hot chocolate, determined to wait till Biff Rogers called or came back to the house to tell them what had happened. It was a long, long wait, and Linda spent much of the time staring off into space, trying to make sense out of what they'd overheard and what had happened.

She jumped nervously when the phone rang. Van Kingsley answered it, then handed the receiver to Elaine. "It's Biff," he said.

The conversation was fairly long and as she watched Aunt Elaine's face, Linda could feel her hope dropping once more. She braced herself for the bad news as Elaine hung up the receiver and turned to face them.

A Timely Trap 15

"What happened?" Van Kingsley asked before Linda could speak.

"They've placed the two men who kidnapped Biff under arrest," Aunt Elaine answered, sinking down at the table again.

"What about the diamonds?" Linda asked. "Did they confess?"

Aunt Elaine shook her head. "All three men deny any knowledge of diamonds and the police, in consultation with the California authorities, claim that they're telling the truth. At least they haven't been able to find anything like that in a thorough search of the men, their cars, and the motel where they've been staying."

"But they have to . . ." Linda protested, her worst fears realized.

"I'm afraid it's worse than that," Aunt Elaine continued.

"What do you mean?" Linda asked. "What could be worse? Without the diamonds, there's no way we can help Andy."

"They've released Wayne. They said they had nothing to hold him on except trespassing here, so . . ." She let it trail off, shrugging. "Biff said that he tried to explain to them that there was more to the case, but the police wouldn't listen." She patted Linda's shoulder consolingly.

"I don't know what to do," Linda moaned.

"Why don't you go to bed, honey," Aunt Elaine suggested. "Biff will be home pretty soon and there's nothing more anyone can do before morning."

Linda wanted to argue, but she was too depressed. She nodded, murmured a few polite words and headed for the stairs to the second floor. She almost wished that she'd slept through everything the way Kathy, Bob, and Larry had—knowing what had happened only made her feel worse. There seemed no hope for Andy now, and she didn't know how they would be able to change that.

It was only when she lay down on her bed that the puzzle began to take shape in her mind. Why had the three men come here? she asked herself. Why take such a chance? What could they have wanted with Chica?

But it wasn't Chica, she realized, remembering what they'd overheard before the dogs came. The men had something, but what . . . ?

Suddenly two pictures filled her mind. First she saw Wayne Upton chased into the horse trailer the night the bunkhouse burned. Then she saw Chica sniffing and pawing at the front wall of the horse trailer.

A flare of hope brought her bolt upright in bed, knocking a book off the nightstand. "What . . . what's going on?" Kathy asked sleepily.

"I think I know where the diamonds are," Linda told her.

"What?" Kathy's sleepiness vanished. "What are you talking about?"

"I'll tell you in a minute," Linda promised, dressing even as she spoke. "I'm going to wake up Bob and Larry. We have to get out to the horse trailer. Get dressed." Linda left Kathy babbling questions as she hurried down the hall to rouse the boys.

Only when they were all safely outside the house and headed for the parking garage did Linda tell the others all that had happened earlier. Their response to the news was just as hers had been, despair at the seeming end of their hope of helping Andy.

"So what are we doing out here?" Bob demanded. "What's going on?"

Linda took a deep breath. "I think the diamonds are hidden in the horse trailer," she said as calmly as she could.

"Oh, come on," Larry began, "why in the world would . . ."

"It's the only thing that makes sense," Linda went on. "Don't you see? There has to be a reason why Upton and his buddies came out here. They weren't looking for Chica—they were looking for the trailer. They just figured that it would be somewhere near our horses."

"He must have had them with him the night of the fire," Bob gasped.

Linda nodded. "Uncle Biff chased him into the horse trailer, and then you searched him and his car, didn't you? He had to ditch them somewhere."

Bob nodded, a grin brightening his face as the pieces fell into place.

"And Chica acted so strange when we first got here," Linda continued. "Maybe she was trying to tell us there was something strange in the trailer."

"A horse that can smell stolen diamonds?" Larry teased. "You should rent her to the police."

"I know it isn't that," Linda retorted, "but the diamonds might be in something that has Beak-nose's scent on it. She'd react to that."

Bob nodded. "We know the ghost was there just before the fire and Chica has plenty of reason to hate him."

They reached the big garage and went in, turning on the lights. Since the horse show was over, a number of the trailers that had been stored there were gone, but theirs stood waiting just where they'd left it. They all hurried to it. Then everyone stopped and Bob waved Linda forward. "It's your theory," he said. "You should have the honour of looking first."

Linda clambered inside the trailer on Chica's side, remembering that she'd seen Wayne Upton in the same stall. There was disappointingly little to see. A few wisps of hay were caught in the barricade, several horsehairs of various colours were dangling from the rougher spots of the combination of wood and metal, but nowhere was there a sparkle of diamonds.

After several minutes, Bob entered the other side of the trailer and began his own search. But peer and pry as they would, there was simply nothing to be seen in the trailer. Blinking back tears, Linda stepped out of the trailer. "I . . . I guess I was wrong," she admitted.

Bob joined her, but no one made a move towards the door. Bob frowned. "Did you say that Upton was released tonight?" he asked.

Linda nodded.

"Well, maybe I'm crazy, Sis, but I still think you're right."

"What do you mean?" Linda asked.

"Your theory makes sense. In fact, it's the only thing that does."

"So what do we do about it?" Larry asked.

Bob looked around. "I think we should turn off the lights and stay here, give our friend Upton a chance to come for the diamonds. If he's the kind of man I think he is, he'll show up here tonight, and then take off for good before his friends get out."

"Maybe we should call the police," Kathy suggested timidly.

"To guard an empty horse trailer?" Bob asked. "I don't think they'd be interested. Besides, we don't want to take any chances of scaring him off. We have to have the diamonds if we're going to clear Andy, and this just could be our only chance to get them."

"I'm with you," Larry said, hurrying across the room to turn off the lights. "Who needs sleep?"

The huge room was eerie, with only the light that filtered in from the small windows on each side. But once their eyes adjusted, they were able to cross to one of the Kingsley trailers and hide themselves inside it. Time inched by as they waited, uncomfortable and fighting sleep.

The silence around them was so deep that they were afraid to even whisper, and when the door finally opened, the sound of it startled them more than a gunshot. Linda held her breath, afraid that the lights would flash on and reveal them, but the only light was a small torch. It was enough, however, to reveal Wayne Upton's intent expression as he crossed the room towards the trailer.

Linda tensed, ready to leap out and confront him, but Bob's hand was firm on her arm, holding her back. Upton climbed into the trailer, moving to the front. He bent down and pushed up on the boards beneath the mangers. There was a grating sound followed by a low chuckle.

"Guess you're all mine, little sparklers," he gloated. "I found the loose board and I've got you now. Old Al won't be able to keep you tucked into his shirt anymore, but where he's going he ain't going to need any diamonds."

"You aren't going to need them either," Bob snarled, moving past Linda with Larry at his side. "Get Uncle Biff and the police," he called as he and Larry tackled the startled wrangler, knocking him to the ground, where the two of them were able to hold him without too much difficulty.

The next hour was a blur of questions, policemen, and explanations; and it was nearly dawn before the weary foursome were sent off to their beds, exhausted but relieved. The diamonds had been recovered from the small leather pouch that Al Lynch, the beak-nosed man, had put them in, and the Nevada police had assured them that word of their recovery would be sent immediately to the California authorities holding Andy Greer.

The sun was shining brightly when Linda awoke at last. For a moment she didn't know what had happened, but then the whole crazy night filled her mind and she sat up, stretching and yawning. It was almost noon and she was starving.

A lavish brunch greeted the four young people when they went downstairs, and as they filled their plates, Uncle Biff asked, "Are you ready for the full story now?"

"Of course," Linda answered. "What have you found out?"

"Well, I just talked to one of the officers who was here last night and he told me that Wayne broke down and did some talking."

"You mean he confessed?" Bob asked.

"Better than that," Uncle Biff answered, "he explained why they were trying to destroy Shadow Canyon."

"Why?" Kathy asked. "What possible reason could they have had for hating nice people like you?"

"It didn't have anything to do with us," Elaine answered. "I mean as people. It was the ranch."

"The ranch?" Linda shook her head in confusion. "What does the ranch have to do with the diamond theft?"

"It's a confused story," Uncle Biff admitted, "but it seems that Al Lynch, Wayne, and the other man were sent out here to locate and purchase a piece of property for some powerful people back East. They chose the Shadow Canyon Ranch. Evidently, they sent pictures and got approval of the ranch, but then when they came to close the deal, they found out the ranch had already been sold to us."

"But couldn't they just look for another ranch?" Bob asked. "Yours is nice, but . . ."

Uncle Biff laughed. "You don't have to be tactful," he said. "I realize the place isn't that unique, but I suspect that some money had already changed hands—or perhaps they'd spent it and lied to their employers. Anyway, they decided to drive us off the ranch, probably assuming that they'd be able to buy it at a better price if they did."

Aunt Elaine sighed. "They don't know how close they came to being right."

"So where do the diamonds come in?" Linda asked.

"They were supposed to pay for the ranch," Uncle Biff replied. "It was a desperation move on their part. Beak-nose was just hanging around the area when he spotted Mrs Barker wearing them. He followed her, watched her, and finally stole them."

"That's it?" Linda asked. "That's the whole story?"

Biff nodded. "Except for their trying to blame Andy. Beak-nose found Andy's bankbook when he was planting the loose diamond in his room. He's the one who made the deposit. He was right about its making Andy look guilty."

"What about Andy?" Bob asked.

"He'll be free and waiting for us when we get back home tonight," Biff replied. "I spoke with Mr O'Roarke and convinced him that the resort owed Andy a bit more than an apology for all he's suffered. He'll have his job back, be paid for the days he's missed, and he's also getting several vacation days, starting today. He'll be spending them with the four of you at Shadow Canyon."

"Oh, Uncle Biff!" Bob and Linda threw themselves on him, hugging him and thanking him for all he'd done to help their friend.

"Hey, how else can we thank you for saving our business?" Uncle Biff asked, a little embarrassed. "After all, you did solve my mystery and catch the ghost."

"I guess we did," Linda admitted with a grin. "I'm so glad."

"And," Uncle Biff added, "you and Chica d'Oro certainly were wonderful representing our ranch!"

Linda just smiled, thinking of her beautiful golden filly.

Armadas are chosen by children all over the world. They're designed to fit your pocket, and your pocket money too – and they make terrific presents for friends. They're colourful, exciting, and there are hundreds of titles to choose from – thrilling mysteries, spooky ghost stories, hilarious joke books, brain-teasing quizzes and puzzles, fascinating hobby books, stories about ponies and schools – and many, many more. Armada has something for everyone.

Armada